BUILDING A PLEX SERVER WITH RASPBERRY PI

BRIAN SCHELL

Building a Plex Server with Raspberry Pi 3 or 4

Copyright 2020 by Brian Schell.

All Rights Reserved. No part of this publication may be reproduced, stored in a retrieval system, or transmitted, in any form or in any means – by electronic, mechanical, photocopying, recording or otherwise – without prior written permission.

Raspberry Pi, Plex, and other products mentioned within are trademarks owned by their respective companies. This book is not affiliated in any way with any group mentioned.

Written and designed by: Brian Schell
brian@brianschell.com

ISBN: 9798615089121
Version Date: February 18, 2020

CONTENTS

1. Introducing Plex and the Pi   1
2. Required Hardware   5
3. Setting up the Hardware   9
4. Setting Up the Plex Media Server Software   35
5. Importing media   61
6. Configuring the Plex Media Server   69
7. Backing up Your SD Card   77
8. Backing Up Your Hard Drive(s)   81
9. Using the Plex Media Server   83
10. Conclusion   93

About the Author   95
Also by Brian Schell   97

1

INTRODUCING PLEX AND THE PI

What is Plex?

Plex is what is known as a media server. You can put movies, music, photos, and other media files on it, and it has all the tools you need to organize, play, watch, and otherwise access that media. Once you have set up a dedicated media server device, you can stream media to your TV, tablets, phones, and other devices, inside your home or even elsewhere through the Internet.

What is a Raspberry Pi?

This product with a silly name is actually a pocket-sized computer. This little box that fits in your pocket is as powerful as any computer you could buy ten years ago. That doesn't sound particularly impressive, but considering the tiny size and price of the Pi, it really is. Although you can set up a spare full-sized computer as your Plex server, a Raspberry Pi (RPI) is more than good enough, and the whole system, bought new with everything you need, will only run you around $50, so it's much less expensive than buying a full-sized computer, probably even cheaper than buying most used PCs.

This book will focus on setting up a Raspberry Pi computer, installing and configuring the Plex software on it, and getting your media into the new system.

What's the catch?

Well, the "trick" is that the Raspberry Pi computer runs Linux rather than Windows or MacOS, so it may require some learning to set up and use. That's the point of this book: to get you from knowing absolutely nothing about Linux or the Raspberry Pi to having a fully-working media server. The only other point of contention is that you must supply the media files, which brings us to our next point...

Is This Legal?

Many people have heard about Plex and jump to the assumption that it's some kind of illegal pirate-streaming-hacker thing. It's not. Plex is a legitimate media server app created by the German company, Plex GmbH. It'll serve up whatever you put into it. Any confusion concerning legality usually revolves around the specific media that is served. Plex Media Server is just software: it doesn't come with any movies, music, or anything of the sort, legal or otherwise-- You have to provide the files containing the media.

You can legally convert your own DVDs, Blu-Ray movies, photographs, and music CDs for use with the system just fine, and you can also download many thousands of public domain movies from sites like Archive.org for free as well.

On the other hand, there are vast numbers of "pirate" sites out there that offer everything from the latest Star Wars movie to the latest season of Westworld. There's nothing illegal about using Plex unless you start getting your *media* illegally, which ought to be obvious. If you want to stay legal, avoid pirate sites. That said, you *can* use Plex to play any media file, regardless of where it came from.

2

REQUIRED HARDWARE

OK, that all sounds good, so what do we need to buy to make this work? Not so much, really. You can go two ways:

Raspberry Pi 4 system:

- Raspberry Pi Model 4 system board ($35-$55 depending on RAM size)
- Some kind of enclosure or case made for the model 4 system ($6 and up)
- 5.1V / 3.0A DC output power supply with micro-USB plug ($8)
- Micro SD Card with 16GB capacity or more ($6)

Raspberry Pi 3B+ System:

- Raspberry Pi Model 3B+ system board (under $35)
- 3.5A Power supply with micro-USB plug ($7)
- Micro SD Card with 16GB capacity or more ($6)
- Some kind of enclosure or case made for the 3B+ system ($6 and up)

And also, for either system:

- One or more externally-powered hard drives to hold media files, the bigger, the better.
- A PC or Mac computer that can access the SD Card for setup.

Optional extras

- HDMI Cable
- Ethernet cable
- Keyboard
- Powered Hub

Pi Notes:

Let's start with the Pi. The current model of Raspberry Pi, as of this writing, is the Raspberry Pi 4. The 3B+ was the version available immediately before the 4 came out. Either of these are fine for this project, but I would strongly recommend against going with anything older than these two models. The 3B+ board is only available in one RAM size, but the model 4 has options for 1MB, 2MB, or 4MB of RAM. Any of these RAM sizes are fine if you only want to build a Plex Media Server. But if you think you may want to use the device for something else in the future, the larger models don't add much to the price, so you may want to consider getting a bigger one. Again, the large-memory version is not necessary for just a Plex server.

Case Notes:

The Pi 3B+ and 4 are *not* the same size or shape, so they require different cases. A cheap case for either can run as low as six dollars. With the 3B+, a cheap case is probably fine, as this model doesn't heat up very much. On the other hand, the model 4 is known for running very hot, and it's almost a necessity to get a case with a built-in fan or some kind of enhanced heat sink. My preferred case for either model is the **Flirc case**, available at most retailers that carry Pi accessories for around $16. The benefit of this case is that it's all-aluminum, and the case itself acts as one big heatsink. With a heat sink, there are no moving parts to wear out and no break-downs to worry about. They just work, reliably and for the long-term.

Power Supply Notes:

The power supply for the 3B+ is essentially the same as an Android phone charger. It uses the micro-USB interface and the same voltage as an Android phone, so you may already have a charger that works with the Pi, or maybe not, since some phones may not have the necessary wattage. The Pi model 4 uses a power supply with a USB-C type connector. Either way, it's probably safest to simply purchase the dedicated power supply made for the Pi for around 7 or 8 dollars.

Micro SD Card Notes:

The Micro SD Card is what the Raspberry Pi uses to hold the operating system and the Plex software. The operating system and Plex software can easily fit (minimally) on an 8GB card, but the data files that Plex uses can get fairly big, so I would recommend getting at least a 16GB ($6) or larger card. Personally, I started with a 16GB card and soon found I needed more. Now, I have a 64GB (around $11) card, and I don't foresee a need to go bigger than that.

Also Needed for Setup:

In the beginning, in order to set everything up, you'll need a working computer that has a port, adapter, or dongle that can read and write to the MicroSD Card you are going to use. You'll download the operating system, write it to the MicroSD card, and then use that card in the Pi. Once you've done this, you don't need the other computer anymore.

Also, in order to set up the Pi the first time, you'll need a keyboard and monitor for the Pi. The model 4 has a Micro-HDMI port, while the model 3B+ uses a regular HDMI cable to plug the monitor into the Pi, so be careful to buy the right cable. A mouse is not needed the way we'll be setting this up. Again, once the system is set up and working, you don't need these things anymore.

3

SETTING UP THE HARDWARE

Step 1: Download the Software Image

Initially, we'll need to download the operating system software and install it on the MicroSD card. This will require a separate computer running Windows, Mac, or Linux. If you really can't make that work, there are many places that will sell you a pre-loaded MicroSD card with the software already installed; a simple Google search for "MicroSD Card Raspian" will help you find a source in your country.

You will need a MicroSD Card and an adaptor/dongle to fit the card into whatever slot your computer has.

There are many distributions, or "brands" of Linux that are easily available. Two of the most popular are Raspbian and Ubuntu. Both of these focus on different things: Raspbian is the "official" operating system of the Raspberry Pi. Ubuntu, on the other hand, is a much heavier, more full-featured operating system that runs well on desktop systems and professional servers. Raspbian is faster and more efficient on the Pi, while Ubuntu is a bit more standardized with professionals and includes more built-in software, but it is also slower.

Ubuntu:

The current version of Ubuntu as of this writing is 18.04, which was released in April of 2018. That sounds "old" (now that we're in 2020), but Ubuntu has an update system in place where they offer something called LTS, or "Long-Term Support" edition of their operating system. They guarantee support for an LTS version for up to four years. The downside of this is that they only release a new version every *two* years. So, there won't be a new LTS edition until April of 2020. There's also a version that is released every 6 months that contains newer, more cutting-edge software, but doesn't get the long-term support of their LTS version.

Ubuntu can be found at

```
https://wiki.ubuntu.com/ARM/RaspberryPi
```

Raspbian:

Raspbian, on the other hand, is released on an irregular schedule whenever enough changes accumulate. The latest version, as of this writing, is called "Buster" (September of 2019). If you want the cutting edge, most "official" version of the Raspberry Pi operating system, this is the one to use.

Both Ubuntu and Raspbian use similar commands in their setups, so which you choose is up to you. My own system runs Raspbian, simply because that's created by the Raspberry Pi foundation, and, at least in theory, should get new features first.

I will be focusing on **Raspbian** in this book, but most of these steps are the same in Ubuntu. One of the great things about the Raspberry Pi is that for the cost of a second Micro SD Card, you can switch back and forth very quickly. Why not try both?

Raspbian can be found at

```
https://www.raspberrypi.org/
downloads/raspbian/
```

Note on which version to download:

You will see on Raspbian's download page that they offer three different versions:

- Raspbian Buster with desktop and recommended software
- Raspbian Buster with desktop
- Raspbian Buster Lite

Of course, by the time you read this, "Buster" may have been replaced by something newer. Still, three versions will be offered. The difference between the three versions lies in how much software you end up getting, and you can see the download sizes (on the website, but not shown here because they vary almost monthly) decrease for each of these three options. The first version is a full desktop experience, with a user interface like Windows and Mac, including a web browser, office software, etc. The middle version gives you the same basic desktop, but leaves out the office software, and the third version is a scaled-down, text-only operating system that looks like an "old-timey" Unix system.

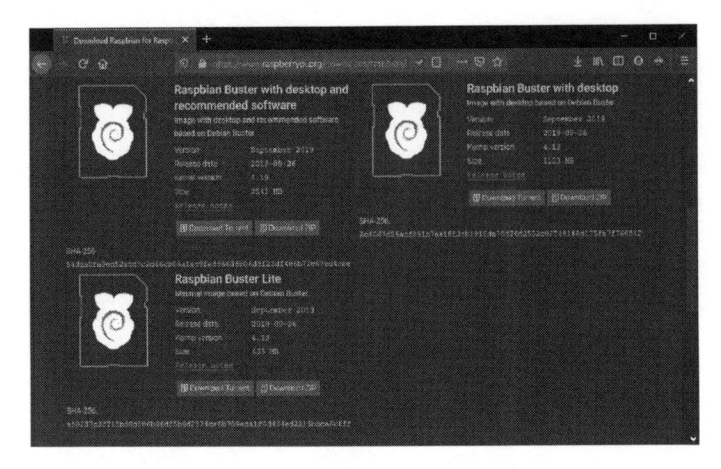

We want the "Raspian Lite" for this project

The truth is, any of these versions will work fine, but if your Pi is going to be a dedicated Plex server and do nothing else, the smallest, third option would be most efficient. There's less to keep updated, less chance of a bug creeping in, and less space used. If you know of some reason to go the full desktop route, then go ahead, but if not, then use the "Lite" version. The remainder of the book will discuss the Lite version, but the steps should be the same on all of them-- it's just that the "bigger" versions add stuff that we don't need for a Plex server.

Step 2: Burn to SD Card

Balena Etcher

The next piece of software that we'll need is a special utility to copy the operating system to the MicroSD Card and make it bootable. If you've copied files onto SD cards before, you might be wondering why this is necessary. It's because *this* SD card must be bootable into a new operating system, which is more complicated than simply copying the file onto the card. The easiest application I've found to do this is **Balena Etcher**, usually just referred to as *Etcher*. There are versions available for Windows, Mac, and Linux, so wherever you're coming from, they make a version for you.

Balena Etcher can be found at:

`https://www.balena.io/etcher/`

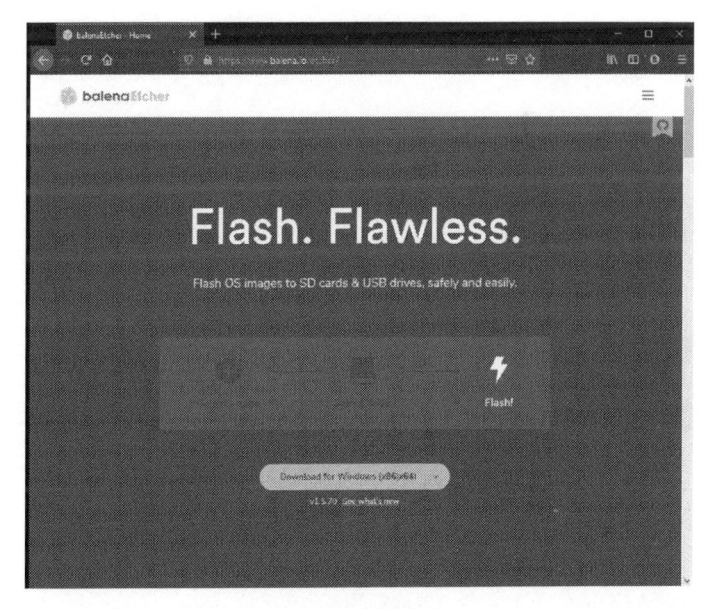

The Balena.io Website

Note: It is also possible to create an SD card image from the command line from MacOS or Linux, but it is complex, and actually impossible from Windows. For the sake of maximum compatibility and simplicity, I'm going to stick with using Etcher here, since it looks and works the same on all three major systems. If you simply *must* do it from the command line for some reason, the official documentation can be found here:

```
https://www.raspberrypi.org/documentation/
installation/installing-images/README.md
```

The process of creating a bootable microSD card with Etcher is simple once you have the above ingredients. Download one of the operating system files, either Ubuntu or Raspbian. Whichever you choose, you'll end up downloading one large **.zip** file.

Once that's done, launch Etcher:

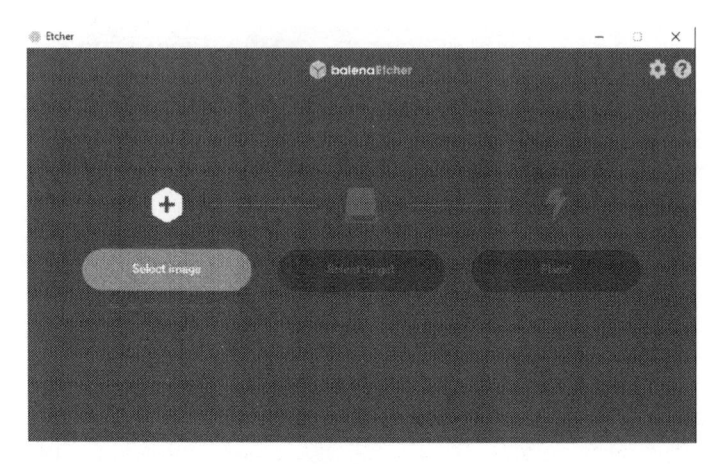

Balena Etcher main screen

There are three buttons and icons. Click the one on the left, and it will allow you to choose a disk image. This is either the single large *Raspbian* or *Ubuntu* file you just finished downloading.

Insert a MicroSD card into the computer. You may need to use an adaptor, dongle, or hub to make it fit; this depends on your machine. Once the computer recognizes the card, click on Etcher's middle icon to select the card. **Make absolutely sure not to select the wrong disk, as you can delete your computer's hard drive if you aren't careful!** Make sure the description of the drive looks right and also compare the drive's reported size to what you think it is. Note that anything on the SD card will be erased in this process, so back up anything that's on there that you wish to save.

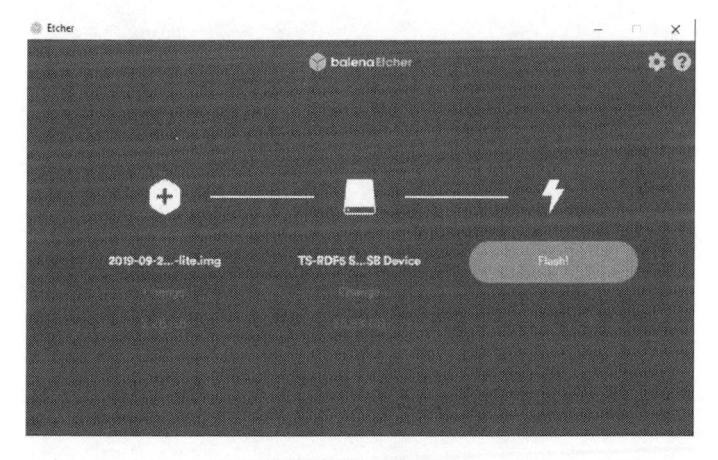

Balena Etcher ready to flash!

When you're done selecting the operating system file and the target drive, then click on the third icon, labeled "Flash!" This will begin the process of formatting the MicroSD Card and copying the operating system onto it. This process may take five to ten minutes depending on how fast your computer is, how fast the card is, and so forth.

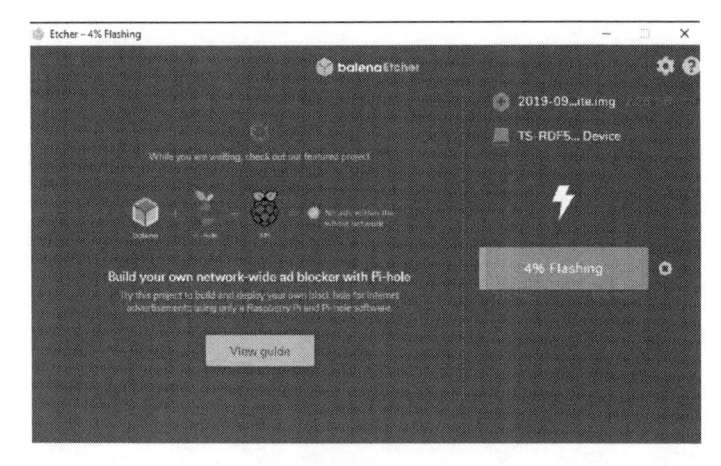

Balena Etcher flashing in process

Once the process has completed, Etcher will tell you that it has flashed the card successfully, or perhaps it will give you an error message. If there's an error, follow Etcher's suggestions to figure out what the problem is. Assuming the process worked, you can eject the card and proceed to assembling your Pi.

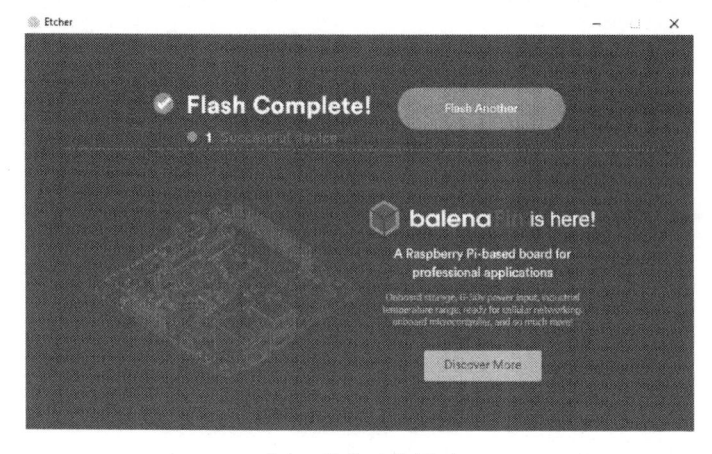

Balena Etcher is finished

Step 3: Assembling the Pi Hardware

Assuming you have purchased or scrounged all the necessary pieces, assembling the Raspberry Pi is very easy, as it should be obvious from looking at the various ports where all the cables should go.

1. Insert your Raspberry Pi motherboard into your case and assemble it using whatever instructions come with the case you have chosen. If your case came with some form of heat sink, be careful not to get fingerprints on either the top of the processor or the bottom of the heat sink and use any thermal compound that came with the set. If it includes a fan, hook up the wires as instructed.
2. Slide the MicroSD Card (with the operating system already installed per the previous section) into the slot on the underside of the Raspberry Pi.
3. Plug in the HDMI to HDMI cable (or HDMI to Micro-HDMI cable for the RPI 4) into the monitor and the RPi.
4. Plug in the keyboard into any of the four USB ports. If you have other USB items, I would recommend sticking with only the keyboard for now; add other peripherals after everything else is working. It's *probably* OK to use a Bluetooth keyboard at this stage, as these should be detected on startup. In the rare chance that the Pi doesn't recognize your Bluetooth device, then a wired keyboard may be needed to get the settings configured.
5. Plug in the ethernet cable between your Pi and your router *if* you don't plan to use Wi-Fi. If you do plan to use Wi-Fi, then this is not needed. Keep in

mind that streaming your media files uses a lot of network bandwidth, so an ethernet connection is the better choice, as it'll increase reliability and also not tie up your Wi-Fi while you watch movies.
6. Plug the monitor into the wall outlet or surge protector.
7. Plug the Raspberry Pi power adaptor into the wall outlet as well.
8. The final step, after everything else, is to plug the power supply into the Pi. The Raspberry Pi itself does not have an on/off switch, so applying power will start the boot process immediately. If your power supply does come with a switch or button, then turn it on now.

At this point, your monitor should show a colorful "test pattern," then clear the screen and show a number of raspberry icons at the top of the screen. After this, a bunch of status messages and text may scroll up the screen.

First-Time Raspbian Setup

As mentioned earlier, we're going to be focusing on the Raspbian distribution from here out. Ubuntu will be very similar, but not exactly the same, as what's shown here.

Assuming you got past the test pattern and the "raspberries," you'll briefly see a message pop up, saying "Resized root filesystem. Rebooting in 5 seconds..." This is normal, but you will only see this message on the *very first boot*, and once this is done, you won't see it again. The Linux system as downloaded takes up one or two gigabytes of space on the SD card; this will boot, but doesn't leave you any work space

Building a Plex Server with Raspberry Pi

for files or software. Resizing the root filesystem is an automatic process that expands the filesystem so that it can use the whole card.

During the bootup process, a ton of system messages will scroll past. Unless you see nothing but errors, these are fine to ignore. Eventually, you will wind up at the Raspbian login screen:

```
Raspian GNU/Linux 10 raspberrypi tty1

raspberrypi login: _
```

The default user for the system is:

Login/Username = **pi**

Password = **raspberry**

Once you have logged in, you should end with a welcome message and a blinking Linux command prompt:

```
Linux raspberrypi 4.19.75-v71+ #1270 SMP
Tue Sep 24 18:51:41 2019 armv71

The programs included with the Debian
GNU/Linux system are free software; the
exact distribution terms for each program
are described in the individual files in
/usr/share/doc/*/copyright.

Debian GNU/Linux comes with ABSOLUTELY NO
WARRANTY. to the extent permitted by
applicable law.
```

```
pi@raspberrypi: $
```

Your operating system is now installed. Now it's time to get it usable!

Changing the Username and Password

The first thing we need to do is deal with a basic security issue. First, we will change the password for the default user. As mentioned above, the default is user **pi** and that user's password is **raspberry**. Since this is the same username and password for *every* default Raspbian install, it's a very good idea to change the password. This user has superuser access and has the ability to delete and change literally anything, so make the password something hard to guess.

At the command prompt, type

```
passwd
```

and follow the prompts. The initial password is "raspberry," but for your new password, you can enter just about anything.

We're going to install the Plex server as the user "pi," so we don't need to add any users right now. If, for some reason, you do want to add more users, you can use the command:

```
adduser
```

and follow the prompts. The only required fields for this command are the new person's username and the password. Again, for a basic Plex Media server, you don't need additional Linux users. You *can* have multiple Plex users, but that's done later.

Setting Up Wi-Fi

First, I strongly recommend that you use ethernet for a Plex Server. It's faster, safer, and more reliable than Wi-Fi. If you are going to use ethernet to plug your Pi into your router directly, then you can skip to the next section, as your ethernet connection should have been set up automatically during the operating system install. Ethernet *just works*, there's no process involved to set it up.

Depending on your household setup, you may *need* to use Wi-Fi, so here's how you can [optionally] set that up; it'll just take a few extra steps to get Wi-Fi going.

Note that the Raspberry Pi model 3B+ and model 4 have *both* 2.4GHz and 5.0GHz capabilities available to you. Older models (which aren't really recommended for a Plex server) only have the 2.4 GHz capability. To begin, at command prompt, type:

```
sudo raspi-config
```

Sudo is a command that lets you change the system as a "superuser." We're not really going to cover security any more than necessary in this book, but just remember that it's a safety measure to keep you from breaking the system accidentally. If you ever type a command, and the system tells you that you "don't have permission" to do that, just add `sudo` in front of the command (once you're darned sure you really mean what you typed).

The other part of that command, `raspi-config`, is the name of the main configuration program for most of the system settings you are able to change. The main screen of raspi-config looks like this:

Raspi-config's Main Menu

You can move through the selections using the arrow keys, with the ENTER key to select an option or the TAB key to jump between the list, <Select>, and <Finish>. We're not going to go through all these options, as most don't apply to Plex, but you might learn something by exploring the various menu options.

The option we want right now is #2, "Network Options." Use the arrow keys and hit Enter to select it.

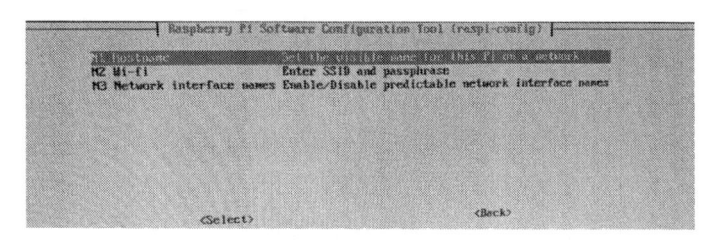

Raspi-config's Network Options Menu

Once you see the Network menu, as in the above screenshot, you should choose option #N2 here for Wi-Fi.

The next dialog box will say "Please enter SSID." The SSID is the name of your local Wi-Fi network. It's the same name you see when you connect to Wi-Fi on your phone. It will *not* auto detect the network name, nor will it automatically populate the field for you: you have to type it in yourself. Be careful to use the proper capitalization, punctuation, and any other unusual characters in the name. Hit Enter when you've got it.

Next, you'll get "Please enter passphrase. Leave it empty if none." This is where you enter your Wi-Fi password. If you mistype either the SSID or passphrase, just use the menus and go back to enter them again. Once you're confident you typed them correctly, use the <Back> option at the bottom to return to the main raspi-config menu, and then use the <Finish> button to return to the command prompt.

The system will ask you if you want to reboot, and you should answer "yes" to this. Once the system reboots, your Wi-Fi should connect automatically from here onward. If it doesn't work, then you most likely typed either the SSID or the password incorrectly, so go back into raspi-config and try again.

Updating the System

It's time to ensure that everything is up-to-date on your system. I know-- you just downloaded it, so how could you have out-of-date software already? Raspian only updates their big "distribution" files every few months, but the individual apps are changed and updated as the need arises. Updating is an easy, two-step process. Type:

```
sudo apt update
```

Note that if you get a bunch of error messages then something is wrong. Wait a minute or two and try again-- it could be something goofy out on the Internet. If the problem persists, then something is probably wrong with either your

Wi-Fi or ethernet connection. Shutdown the system by typing

```
sudo shutdown -h now
```

and the system will shut down. Unplug the Raspberry Pi and then plug it back in to reboot. You may need to reset your router as well, but that's unusual.

Assuming everything works, then the `sudo apt update` command will go out on the Internet and download a list of all the files that make up your system and compare that list to what you have installed. Anything that is newer on the list gets marked for upgrading in the next step. When the "update" command is finished, then type:

```
sudo apt upgrade
```

This command looks at that "update" list and then goes through and downloads and installs everything that has newer versions available. It's a very smart and useful system, and (unlike Windows) you only do it *when you are ready* for updates.

And that's it-- We bought and assembled all the pieces, and then we downloaded and created our boot media. We then set up Wi-Fi, changed our password, updated the system, and ended up with a bare-bones, but still fully working little computer. Keep in mind that since we are "only" building a Plex server, we chose the command-line server version of Raspbian. We could have chosen the full desktop version and run the Raspberry Pi as a low-powered computer with office software, web browsing, and everything. Or maybe that can be your project for another time!

Configuring the Hard Drive(s)

The operating system we just installed went on the microSD card. That microSD card is what the raspberry pie will be using in the future to boot every time you plug it in or reboot the system. Still, microSD cards are relatively slow and don't hold much space, even if you buy a large one.

You're probably going to have far more media than a microSD card can handle, so we need to install one or more large, physical hard drives. This is not as simple as just plugging it in and making it work. Linux requires some configuration to allow the system to see the hard drives and connect the hard drives in a consistent way each time the system is booted. It sounds like it *should* just work, but that's not the way it is. Once we configure things, you should not have to mess with any of this again, but it does require some configuration in the beginning.

Preparing an external data drive involves a bit of work. This section will end with you having a hard drive which will mount automatically when you boot the Pi and can be used for your media files. If you already have a Linux-formatted (i.e. ext4) drive with important data already on it that you wish to use as a data drive, you can skip to step 15. If you have a blank drive, or want to re-task a drive with "junk" already on it, then start right here:

1. Plug in the hard drive to power (if necessary) and to the Raspberry Pi.

2. Power up the Raspberry Pi and wait for the system to boot from the SD card as always.

At the command prompt, type

```
sudo fdisk /dev/sda
```

Because you are using the *fdisk* command in superuser mode (sudo), it *may* ask for your password. After you enter the password, you should see:

```
Welcome to fdisk (util-linux 2.33.1)

Changes will remain in memory only, until
you decide to write them. Be careful before
using the write command.

Command (m for help):
```

The command *fdisk* is a very powerful tool for creating, deleting, partitioning, and otherwise changing hard drive attributes. If you are curious about the options, press m to see the menu choices.

3. Press p to *print* the partition table. The numbers will all probably be somewhat different, but the output should look something like this:

```
Command (m for help): p
Disk /dev/sda: 465.8 GiB, 500107862016
bytes, 976773168 sectors
Disk model: Portable SSD T5
Units: sectors of 1 * 512 = 512 bytes
Sector size (logical/physical): 512 bytes /
```

```
512 bytes

I/O  size  (minimum/optimal):  512  bytes  /
33553920 bytes

Disklabel type: dos

Disk identifier: 0x8e1d0b09


Device Boot Start End Sectors Size Id Type

/dev/sda1 2048 976770112 976768065 465.86G
7 HPFS/NTFS/exFAT


Command (m for help):
```

From the above, I can see that my drive is an external SSD drive with 465.8GB, and is currently set up with one partition, */dev/sda1*. We don't need to worry about most of the other information for now. Our goal for right now is to delete those old partitions and create a single large partition to replace them.

4. Press d for "delete partition"

If your drive has multiple partitions, you will be asked to choose which one you want to delete:

```
Partition number (1,2, default 2):
```

Again, you may only have one partition, or more than two, or maybe none at all. The goal here is to delete *all* the partitions. In my case, I only had one partition, and when I pressed d to delete, I got the message "Partition 1 has been deleted"-- it didn't even ask for verification!

After all the partitions are gone, use the p command to print the partition table again. If the previous step worked correctly, there shouldn't be anything listed after "Disk identifier." However many /sda devices you had should all be gone. Again, if you had a new, blank drive, you may not have seen any partitions at all.

5. Use the n command in fdisk to create a new partition.

6. Unless you know some reason you need to do otherwise, choose p to make the new partition *Primary*.

7. Make the new partition "Partition 1" by pressing 1 or hitting the Enter key for the default.

8. Accept the default values for the first and last sectors. This will make the new partition fill the entire hard drive.

9. It may take a few seconds, but you should soon see:

```
Created a new partition 1 of type 'Linux'
and of size 465.7 GiB.
```

Assuming the size given approximates the size of your hard drive, you're doing good. If for some reason, you want to make multiple partitions, you can adjust the previous few steps to accommodate your needs, but for a Plex server, there's no reason to use multiple partitions.

10. When you are done creating partitions, use the w command in fdisk to write changes to the disk. **Nothing you have done so far (with fdisk) is permanent until you**

do this. Once you write your changes, all data, partitions, and everything else will be wiped from the disk, so be sure everything looks good before you commit to this.

11. Press **p** to once again print the list of partitions. It should now look somewhat like this:

```
Command (m for help): p

Disk /dev/sda: 465.8 GiB, 500107862016 bytes, 976773168 sectors

Disk model: Portable SSD T5

Units: sectors of 1 * 512 = 512 bytes

Sector size (logical/physical): 512 bytes / 512 bytes

I/O size (minimum/optimal): 512 bytes / 33553920 bytes

Disklabel type: dos

Disk identifier: 0x8e1d0b09

Device Boot Start End Sectors Size Id Type

/dev/sda1 65535 976773167 976707633 465.7G 83 Linux

Command (m for help):
```

And as you see near the bottom, there is a new device, */dev/sda1* that uses the entire hard drive.

12. We're done with fdisk, so use the **q** command to quit.

13. You will need to reboot the Pi for changes to take effect.

The command `sudo reboot` will make this easy.

14. The new hard drive now has an empty, unformatted partition, but it's not ready to hold any data until we format it. Type:

```
sudo mkfs /dev/sda1
```

This will format the drive with a Linux filesystem. Depending on the size and speed of the drive, this will take some time, but you should be able to watch the progress on your monitor.

15. Now that you have a hard drive that is partitioned and formatted, you will need to create a *mount point* within your regular directory structure. This is a "folder" that represents the external hard drive to the computer. You can put it wherever you want, but I generally just put it in the / (root) directory. Type:

```
sudo mkdir /mydrive
```

This will create a new directory called "mydrive" in the / directory. Now, it might seem more reasonable to name the drive "media" since this is where we're going to be putting our media files, but Linux already has a folder by that name that is used for something else. To avoid confusion, we'll just go with */mydrive*.

Next, the physical hard drive needs to be "mounted" to that mount point. Assuming your hard drive was called *sda1* back in step 11, then you would type the following:

```
sudo mount /dev/sda1 /mydrive
```

Of course, if your disk is something other than */dev/sda1*, or if you used something other than /mydrive, then you should make the appropriate substitutions in the command above.

> 16. You will need to set ownership of the new drive to your user account. For most Plex servers, the user will stay as the default "pi." If you are still logged in as the user "pi" then just type:

```
sudo chown pi:pi -R /mydrive
```

If, however, you set up a different username earlier, then you would use that name here. For example, if you set up the username 'brian,' you would need to change ownership of the drive to that user:

```
sudo chown brian:brian -R /mydrive
```

And now the user *brian* can save and manipulate files in the drive without needing to use sudo all the time. Again, for a basic Plex setup, you don't need to be adding additional users, so adding users just adds unnecessary complexity.

> 17. Test out everything by typing the following:

```
cd /mydrive

touch test.txt

ls
```

The *touch* command simply changes the file date on an existing file, or creates a new, blank file if it doesn't already exist. The *ls* command is for "list structure," the Linux way of showing the files in a directory. It should list:

```
lost+found.  test.txt
```

Lost+found is something that is always generated automatically, but *test.txt* is the file that you just created with the *touch* command. If you see it, then you should be able to save, copy, delete, and otherwise manipulate files within the new drive. If you don't see it, or if you get an error message, then skip back to step 16 and make sure you gave the current user permission to write to the hard drive.

Setting up the External Drive to Mount Automatically

Thought you were done? Nope. But you're getting there!

Now you will need to manually set the system up to automatically mount the external drive every time you boot the system.

1. Type the following:

```
sudo fdisk -l
```

That last character is a lowercase 'L' if you can't tell.

This will list all the various partitions and disks that are available to you. Usually, the external drive will be **at the very bottom of the list.** You need to make note of the "Device" name, for example, **/dev/sda1** or **/dev/sda2** or whatever comes up if you have more than one drive or partition connected.

2. We will now modify one of the main Linux configuration files to recognize the drive at bootup time. We will edit the */etc/fstab* file using the Nano editor. Type:

```
sudo nano /etc/fstab
```

You'll something similar to the following:

```
proc /proc proc defaults 0 0

PARTUUID=6c586e13-01  /boot  vfat  defaults 0 2

PARTUUID=6c586e13-02 / ext4 defaults,noatime 0 1

# a swapfile is not a swap partition, no line here

# use dphys-swapfile swap[on|off] for that
```

The PARTUUID numbers will certainly be different from mine above, but the file should otherwise resemble this closely. Move the cursor to the end of the file and add the following on a blank line:

```
/dev/sda1 /mydrive ext4 defaults,nofail 0 0
```

Substituting */dev/sda1* and */mydrive* with whatever you used in previous steps. Use ctrl-o to save, then ctrl-x to exit Nano; The Nano text editor has some help text at the bottom of the screen if you get lost using it. Once you reboot, the new hard drive should be available to you to use automatically, every time you boot the Pi.

Reboot the system once more:

```
reboot
```

And the system should reboot with the new drive mounted, formatted, and ready to go. If you plan to add more than one drive, just repeat the above steps, and keep in mind that if the first hard drive is named */dev/sda* then the second drive will be named */dev/sdb* and so forth.

4

SETTING UP THE PLEX MEDIA SERVER SOFTWARE

Downloading and Installing Plex

Adding the Plex Repository

We talked earlier about the "lists" that `sudo apt update` went out and looked up for us. The purpose of that command was to do a software update. These same lists, more properly known as "repositories," can be used to install software as well. There are some basic repositories that were included in Raspbian, but you can add others.

Now we will add a repository for the Plex Media Server system. The purpose of doing this is so that in the future, when the Plex software gets updated, your system will automatically know where to look for updates. Type the following very carefully, all as one big, long line:

```
echo deb https://downloads.plex.tv/repo/deb public main | sudo tee /etc/apt/sources.list.d/plexmediaserver.list
```

Hit Enter at the end of all that and then follow this up with:

```
curl https://downloads.plex.tv/plex-keys/PlexSign.key | sudo apt-key add -
```

The first command adds the repository to the system's list of safe places to download updates. The second adds an authorization key to verify that the downloads from that site are authentic. [Please note that the second command does end with a hyphen/dash, that's not a typo]. All of the preceding commands should only need to be done just once.

Once these changes have been made, we need to refresh the list of repositories with:

```
sudo apt update
```

And we're finally ready to install Plex with:

```
sudo apt install plexmediaserver
```

and Plex is installed. The final step is to type:

```
ifconfig
```

at the command prompt, and make note of the Raspberry Pi's IP address. The output from ifconfig will look like this:

```
wlan0:

flags=4163<UP,BROADCAST,RUNNING,MULTICAST> mtu 1500

inet    192.168.0.6    netmask    255.255.255.0 broadcast 192.168.0.255

inet6   fe80::594f:cad3:ff2a:c07e   prefixlen 64 scopeid 0x20<link>
```

```
ether   dc:a6:32:02:b1:56   txqueuelen   1000
(Ethernet)

RX packets 52230 bytes 73794731 (70.3 MiB)

RX errors 0 dropped 0 overruns 0 frame 0

TX packets 24158 bytes 9006450 (8.5 MiB)

TX errors 0 dropped 0 overruns 0 carrier 0
collisions 0
```

The only part that matters is the beginning of the second line, right after "inet." This is your *IP address*, the numerical location for your RPI in the local network in your home or office. It's formatted as four numbers separated by periods. In the example above, the IP address for my Raspberry Pi system is **192.168.0.6**, and this is how we'll access Plex from now on.

Setting up your Raspberry Pi for Remote Access

Most people run their Plex Server "headless," that is, with no monitor or keyboard attached. This makes typing commands a bit of a challenge! Not really, because we can set the Pi up to be able to be accessed from other computers-- or even your smartphone.

Go back into raspi-config by typing

```
sudo raspi-config
```

just as we've done before. This time, select option 5: "Interfacing Options." Use the menu to choose submenu 2 "SSH Enable" and choose "Yes" to enable the server when asked. It's probably best to reboot the system afterwards to make sure the changes take place.

You can then disconnect the keyboard and monitor and place your headless Raspberry Pi somewhere out of the way. You'll obviously still need to be plugged into power, plugged into the hard drive, and probably plugged into your ethernet, but you can unplug the keyboard and the monitor if you want. Actually, it's probably smartest to leave these plugged in until we're actually certain everything works with Plex, but at least in theory, we are done with the keyboard and monitor at this stage.

Now you can access your Raspberry Pi's command prompt from almost any device on your network running some kind of terminal app:

Terminal Apps to use:

- Windows: Download the app *Putty* from https://putty.org/
- Mac or Linux: Use the built-in *Terminal App*
- Android or iPhone: the *Termius App* (See Google Play or IOS App Store)
- iPad: *Termius* or *Blink Shell App* (See App Store)

There are many other possible apps, but these are the ones I have used and am familiar with; others are probably just as good. If you are trying to find an app somewhere, search for a "SSH Terminal app" of some sort.

You will open up one of these terminal apps on some other system and connect it to your Pi and type in commands that way. Note that this process is only for configuring and updating your system later-- you can use much simpler Plex apps to watch your movies and media things, which we'll get to later. If this is a step you'd rather skip, then you always have the option of leaving the Pi connected to a keyboard and screen.

From one of the above Terminal Apps, you can type:

`ssh pi@192.168.0.6`

(or whatever your user name and IP address are)

Then you will be prompted for a password. Once you enter the password for user "pi," you will be at a command prompt on the Pi itself. Typing commands here are executed on the Raspberry Pi, not your local computer; it's like using your device as a remote keyboard and monitor!

Setting up and Importing Your Media Files

Now that the system is all built and the software is ready to go, and now that the Pi can be accessed either from the keyboard and monitor connected to the Pi or remotely from some other system, we can start getting the media files installed.

Supported File Formats

Before we do anything, we need to make sure our media files are something that Plex can understand.

Movies, TV Shows, and Other Video must be in one or more of the following file formats:

- AVI
- MKV
- MOV
- MP4
- WMV

Subtitles for Movies and TV Shows are optional, but can be in the following formats:

- SRT
- SMI
- SSA or ASS
- VTT

Music must be in one or more of the following formats:

- AAC
- ALAC
- E-AC3
- FLAC
- MP3
- M4A
- WAV

Photos:

- Most common image formats are supported

If you have some other format of media, go ahead and try it and see what happens; Plex is surprisingly smart in that it can convert many things on the fly. At the very worst, you may need to download some kind of conversion software to convert your video to one of the above formats.

Note that you can mix and match any or all of these. If you download movies in MP4, AVI, MKV, and MOV formats, you don't need to convert them all to one format. Just use them all, and so long as it's a supported format, Plex will sort it out and it will be

Building a Plex Server with Raspberry Pi

transparent to the user when Plex presents it for viewing.

Media Categories and Organization

First, we need to make a home on our external hard drive for our media files. Plex expects the files you use to be in a certain folder structure. If you just want to throw your various media items into one big folder, Plex will do what it can to make them viewable, but to get the most out of Plex, you'll want to categorize your files in this structure.

On your hard drive, you'll make a directory (or folder) for Movies, another for TV Shows, one for Music, and so forth. Beneath each of these are subfolders for each individual Movie, TV Show, or Album. Beneath these subfolders are individual files for movies, episodes, songs, etc.

Type the following at the command prompt:

```
cd /mydrive

mkdir Movies

mkdir TV

mkdir Music

mkdir Photos

mkdir Other
```

The first command moves us into the hard drive we added, and the other five commands make directories/folders for each of the main media types. Once you have everything set up the way you want, you can change these names and add other folders for special purposes, but for now, let's just go with the basic media types above.

Now before we copy files into these folders, we need to make sure the files are named properly. It's amazing how much fun a Plex system can be if it understands what you've put into it, and the way it understands this is a combination of file names and folder structures.

Movies

Movie files are usually just the name of the movie and the year released. Each individual movie can be placed in a subfolder if you want, or they can just all mix together in the MOVIES folder if you prefer. For example:

```
A Quiet Place (2018).m4a
```

```
Coraline (2009).mkv
```

and so on. Note that spaces in the file names are perfectly fine.

Adding subtitles for movies and TV shows are optional, but if you want them, they must have the exact same filename as the movie, but with an extension of .srt or one of the other acceptable extensions.

```
A Quiet Place (2018).srt
```

```
Coraline (2009).vtt
```

Assuming all your movies are named like this, Plex will be able to look them up on the Internet and download posters, descriptions, ratings, reviews, and other fun information about the movies, which makes the experience far better than just a simple movie viewer.

Music

Under the MUSIC folder, you will create a folder for each specific artist or band. Beneath the artist folder, you create individual folders for each album. Inside each album folder, you place all the individual song files.

```
MUSIC
    Abba
        Ring Ring
            01 - Ring, Ring.mp3
            02 - Another Town, Another Train.mp3
            03 - Disillusion.mp3
            04 - People Need Love.mp3
                (...Other songs from the Ring, Ring album...)
        Waterloo
            01 - Waterloo.mp3
            02 - Sitting In The Palmtree.mp3
            03 - King Kong Song.mp3
            04 - Hasta Manana.mp3
                (...Other songs from the Waterloo album...)
```

Music File/Folder Hierarchy

TV Shows

Make a folder for each unique TV series name. Inside that folder, make a folder for each season for the show (simply named "Season 1", "Season 2", etc.). Then within those season folders, you put the individual episode of that year's shows, usually found in the format:

```
TV
    Land of the Lost
        Season 1
            ...
        Season 2
            Land of the Lost S02E01.mp4
            Land of the Lost S02E02.mp4
            Land of the Lost S02E03.avi
            Land of the Lost S02E04.mkv
            Land of the Lost S02E05.mp4
        Season 3
            ...
```

TV Show Hierarchy

The above example demonstrates the files for the "Land of the Lost" TV series, and the first five episodes of the second season. Note that the file formats do not all have to match; mkv, avi, and mp4 all live together happily so long as the season and episode numbers are set up correctly.

Especially note how the episodes above contain the Season and Episode numbers. S04E12 would represent season (or series) 4, episode number 12. By coding the TV episodes in this manner, Plex can not only play the shows in the correct order, it can also look up stars, plot lines, ratings, and other information for each specific episode.

Again, Plex is quite intelligent about all this, and what I've shown above is not the only way to do it. For another example, the single-season BBC show "Hammer House of Horror":

```
TV
    Hammer House Of Horror
        1.Witching Time.mp4
        2.The Thirteenth Reunion.mp4
        3.Rude Awakening.mp4
        4.Growing Pains.mp4
        5.The House that Bled to Death.mp4
        6.Charlie Boy.mp4
        7.The Silent Scream.mp4
        8.Children of the Full Moon.mp4
        9.The Carpathian Eagle.mp4
        10.Guardian of the Abyss.mp4
        11.Visitor from the Grave.mp4
        12.Two Faces Of Evil.mp4
        13.The Mark of Satan.mp4
```

Alternate TV Hierarchy

This show only ran a single year, so there's no reason to put in the season information. Just by numbering the episodes, they will appear in Plex in the correct order.

Generally speaking, it's easiest to just copy in the files however you get them and see what happens. Most logical file naming conventions will work. If you run into a situation where your shows aren't appearing in Plex, or are playing in the wrong order, or something else strange, then go in and look at changing the filenames. This will usually clear up problems.

Photos

Photos are really easy. Just copy your files in any way that seems reasonable to you. You can put them into folders to organize them by date, or location, or subject, or however you want. Or you can just dump a thousand image files in the main Photo folder and let Plex sort them out. It's up to you!

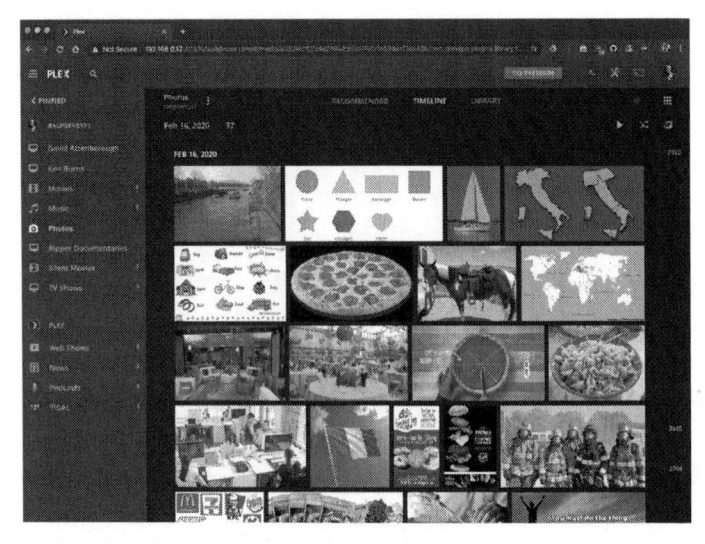

Photos in Timeline View

Other Videos

There's a category of "Other Videos" as well. This is generally intended for things like home movies that are technically video, but without the metadata concerning stars, directors, and stuff like that that only a professional film would have.

Example

Below is my example structure. The main hard drive is called */mydrive* as we set up earlier. Beneath that are folders for MOVIES, MUSIC, TV SHOWS, PHOTOS, and OTHER. Beneath the MOVIES folder are subfolders for *some* of the movies, and inside each of these is the file containing the movie itself, and some of those also have optional subtitle files. Note that not every movie is identical; some have the year, some don't. Some are in folders, and some aren't. Each level of indentation shows a deeper level of subfolders.

```
mydrive  [THE ROOT OF THE HARD DRIVE]
    MOVIES  [FOLDER]
        A Quiet Place (2018)  [SUBFOLDER]
            A Quiet Place.mp4
            A Quiet Place.srt
        Coraline (2009)
            Coraline.avi
            Coraline.srt
        House of 1000 Corpses (2003).mkv
        Psycho.mov
        Psychotica
            Psychotica.wmv
            Psychotica.srt
        The Orphanage (2007)
            Orphanage.mp4
            Orphanage.srt
        The Poughkeepsie Tapes (2007)
            Poughkeepsie Tapes.mov
            Poughkeepsie Tapes.vtt
    MUSIC  [FOLDER]
        Abba  [SUBFOLDER]
            Ring Ring  [SUB-SUBFOLDER]
                01 - Ring, Ring.mp3
                02 - Another Town, Another Train.mp3
                03 - Disillusion.mp3
                04 - People Need Love.mp3
                    Other Individual Songs not all listed
            Waterloo
                14 Individual Songs (not all listed)
            Arrival
                12  Individual Songs (not all listed)
            Voulez-Vous
                14 Individual Songs
            Super Trouper
                12 Individual Songs
        Aqua
            Greatest Hits
                2  Individual Songs
            Aquarium
                11  Individual Songs
            Aquarius
```

```
                    12  Individual Songs
            Megalomania
                    11  Individual Songs
        Blondie
            Greatest Hits
                    11  Individual Songs
            Ghosts of Download
                    13  Individual Songs
TV SHOWS [FOLDER]
        Chernobyl
            5 Individual Episodes
        Hammer House of Horror
            13 Individual Episodes
        Land of the Lost [SUBFOLDER]
            Season 1 [SUB-SUBFOLDER]
                    17  Individual Episodes
            Season 2
                    13  Individual Episodes
            Season 3
                    13 Individual Episodes
PHOTOS
        Various image files in optional subfolders
OTHER
        This is up to you. Put your home movies here.
```

This is a lot to take in, but you can always move or rename files that aren't right; you aren't going to permanently break anything if you mess it up. Plex is actually fairly easy-going about all this, and will often figure out what you mean.

If you need to see Plex's documentation on file names and file structure, here are the links:

```
https://support.plex.tv/articles/cate-
gories/your-media/
```

Eventually, you'll need to get all your media files copied to */mydrive* and filed in one of the media folders. It might seem daunting, but if you just add a dozen or so titles at a time, make sure they show up in Plex, and then add more, it'll get done eventually. And, fortunately, you will only have to do it once.

If you are feeling confident, you can start copying your

media to the Raspberry PI and the media folders right now. If not, you can wait until the section titled "Importing Media Files."

How to Set Up Your Plex Account

Moving to another computer on the same network, open up a web browser and in the URL/Address bar at the top, type in:

```
192.168.0.6:32400/web/
```

another option, which might be easier to remember is:

```
https://app.plex.tv
```

Be sure to substitute your IP number for mine. Put in your IP number and add the :32400/web onto the end of it. Hit Enter, and something like the following should show up:

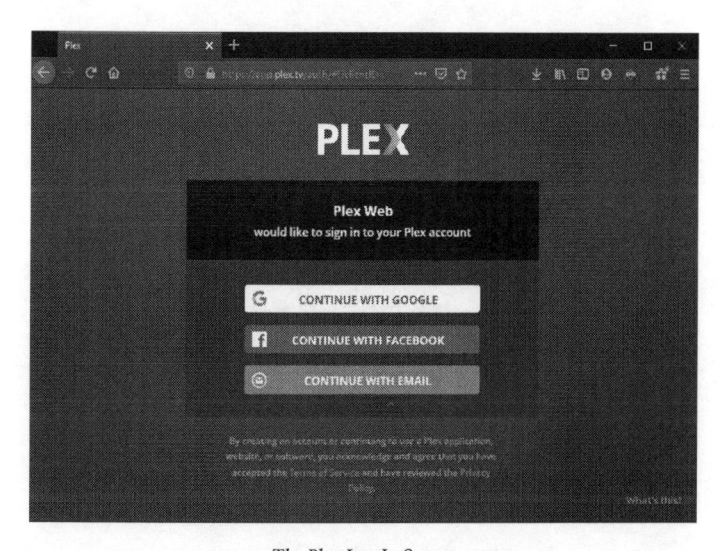

The Plex Log-In Screen

You can set up an account by clicking on one of the three buttons and following the prompts. The three methods are all a little different, so I'll let you work that out on your own. If you choose the EMAIL option, it will ask for an email and a password. Use a real email and make up a new password. Plex will realize that you don't have an account and ask if you want to create one. Do so.

Once Plex has set up your password, you'll be forwarded to a mostly-black login screen where you will enter a four-digit PIN. This will take you to this screen, where you can click on "Got it!" to continue:

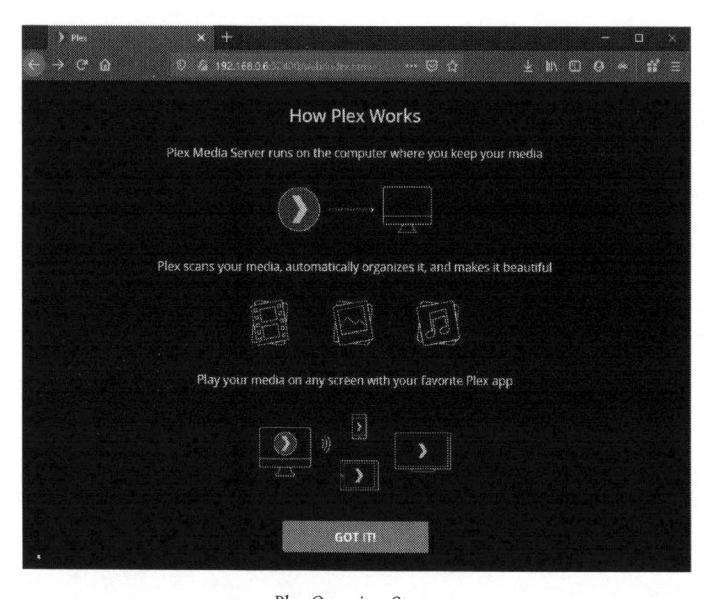

Plex Overview Screen

Note that at no point in the sign-up process should you pay for anything or even need to put in a credit card. There *is* a paid option for Plex that we'll talk about later, but you do **not** need this to get started. If it won't let you proceed without payment, then you probably clicked something you shouldn't have. Start the process over and try differently.

Sure enough though, the very next screen will try to talk us into buying "Plex Pass," something we can worry about later:

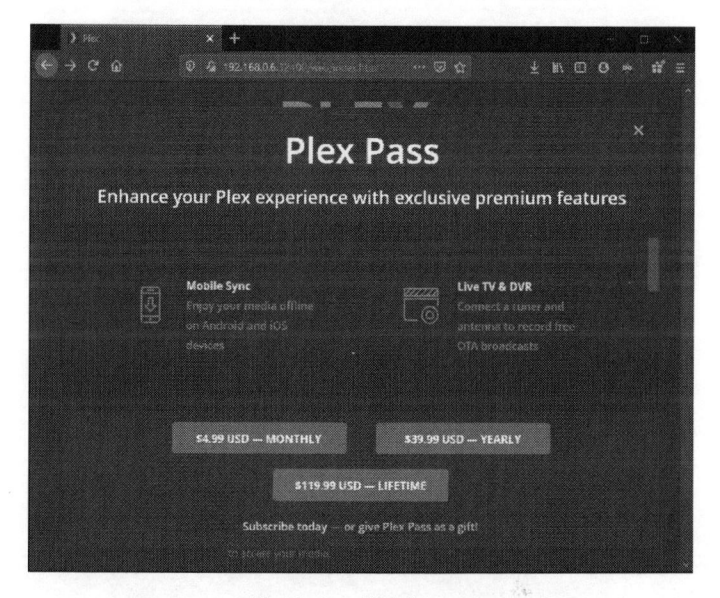

The Plex Pass "Sales" Screen

To make this screen go away, click on the little "X" in the top-right corner of the browser window just to the right of the words "Plex Pass."

Finally, we're getting down to business. Plex should then come up with a "server found" message. It will ask you "Give it a friendly name to help identify it in Plex apps and on your network." and the current name will be "raspberrypi." You can change this to something else if you want, but it's optional. In my case, I just left it at the default.

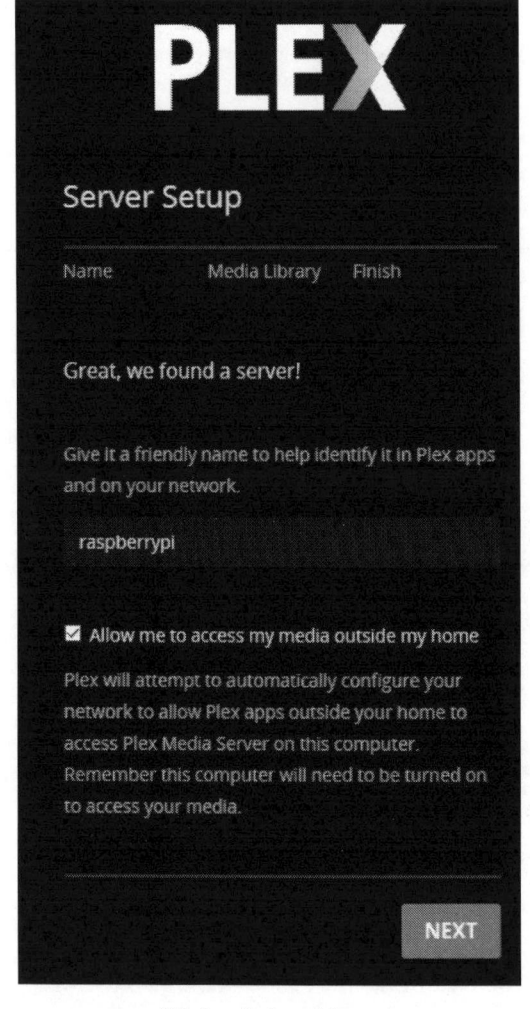

"We Found a Server" Screen

The second important thing on this page is the checkbox for "Allow me to access my media outside my home." Note that accessing your movies and music outside the house via the Internet requires quite a bit of Internet bandwidth. If you are on a limited or capped Internet plan, you may want to think about leaving this off. You can use Plex within your house, through your own Wi-Fi, with no Internet bandwidth usage. If you know you're only going to use Plex around the house, then uncheck this box now. If you do plan on using Plex outside the house, then leave this checked. If you aren't sure, then leave it off; you can turn it on later.

Creating Libraries

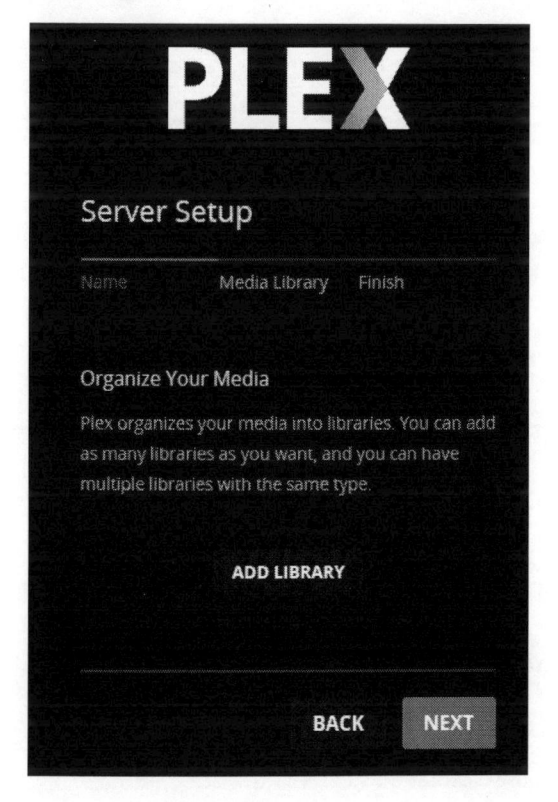

From the screen above, click on "Add Library." The following screen will pop up:

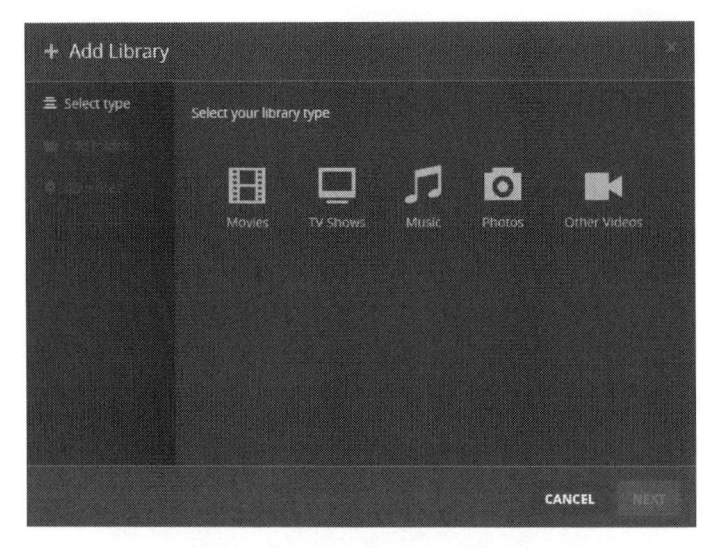

Adding Libraries

OK, now we have to do some planning. Keep in mind that if you do this wrong, it's not hard to redo things later. You will need to sort your media into one of five media types:

- Movies
- TV Shows
- Music
- Photos
- Other Videos

Let's start with movies.

1. Click the movie icon and then choose your language. Choose Next for the next screen.

2. You are now on the screen to "Add folders to your

library" and there is a link to "Browse for media folders." Click this.

3. Now we need to find a place to put our movies. In the following screen, click on "mydrive" or whatever you named your hard drive:

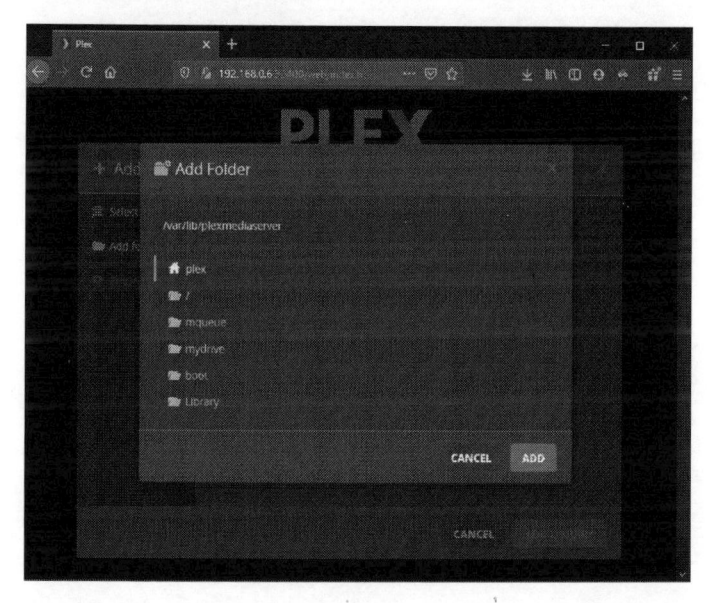

Assigning a Folder to a Library

4. If you made media folders at the end of the last section, you will see them listed here. You might need to scroll down to see them all:

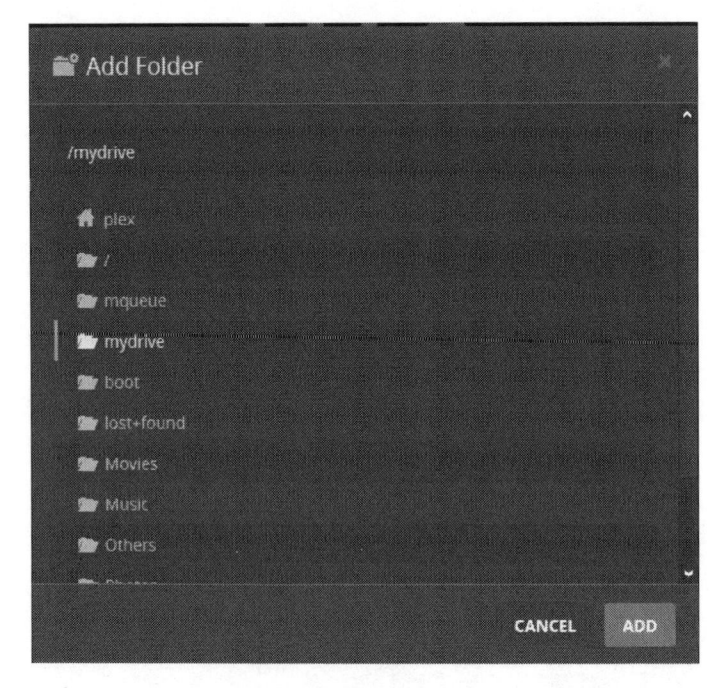

Scroll to find the Desired Folder

5. Choose the folder for Movies. Click the folder for Movies and choose "Add."

6. You will be returned to the "Add folders to your library" screen:

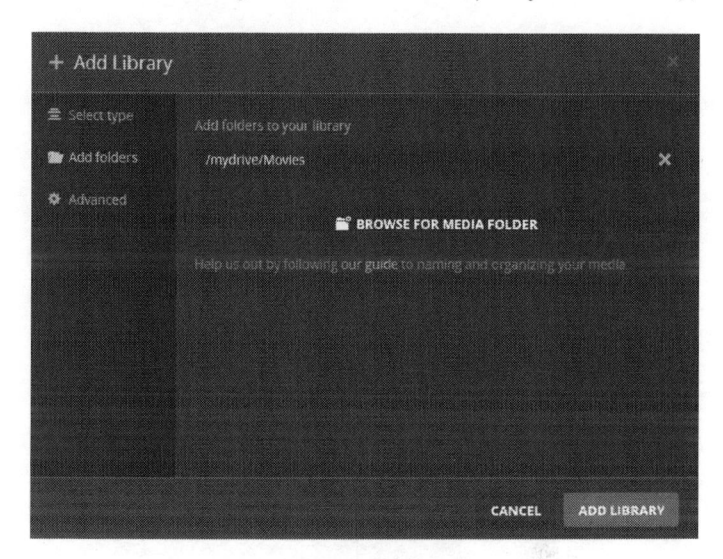

"Add More Folders?"

And now you can do the same steps over again for Music, Photos, TV, and Others. If you know you don't want a certain category, i.e. you aren't going to put any photos in Plex, then you can skip that library if you want. After you've added all the categories you want, you'll see the following screen. If you know you did something wrong, you can click on the pencil icon to edit a category or the red X to delete it and add it again correctly this time:

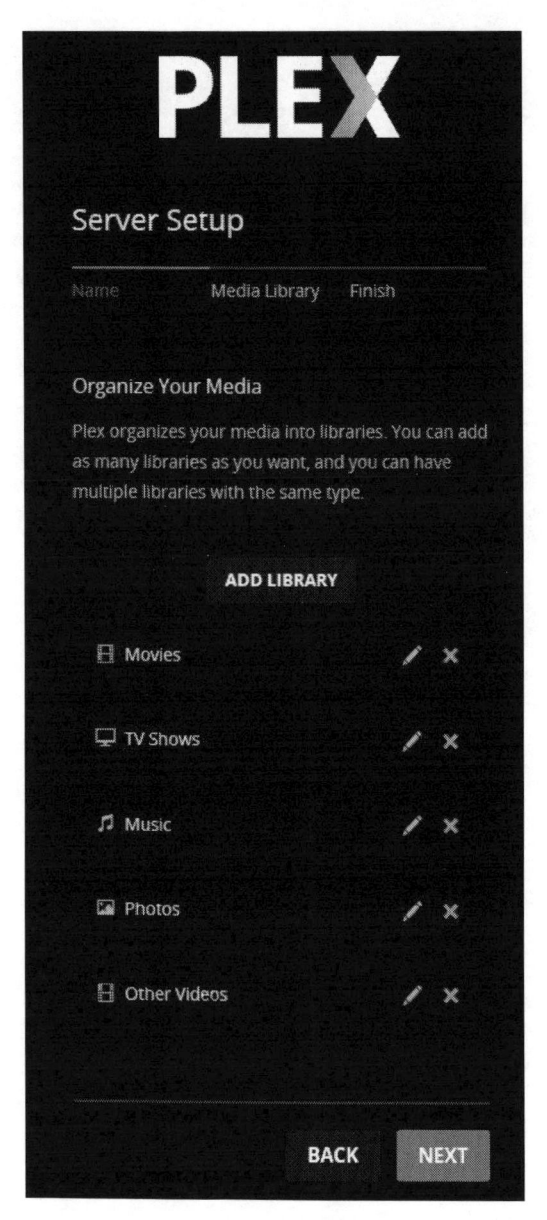

Review or Edit Your Libraries

We're almost done. If you're fairly confident that everything is what you want, then click on "Next," and you'll get a message about downloading Plex Apps. Read through this and then click "Done."

Plex is now fully configured.

If you haven't already added media files, now it's time to do so!

Quick Reference

- Accessing Plex from a web browser on the same network: (Replace with your IP number): **http://192.168.0.6:32400/web** or **https://app.plex.tv**
- If you need to shutdown the Plex server, type **sudo shutdown -h now**
- To reboot the system, then simply type: **reboot**
- To upgrade the system and the Plex software type these two commands:

    sudo apt update

    sudo apt upgrade

5
IMPORTING MEDIA

We've described the file formats that Plex understands, and then we talked about the folder structure and file naming conventions that Plex prefers. The one important thing we haven't spoken about is "how do you get those files onto the hard drive we set up?" There are three common ways to do it.

1. Copy from the command line manually.
2. Copy from the terminal using a shell app like Midnight Commander.
3. Use an FTP app from a "regular" computer to transfer files..

Manual Copy from the Command Line (The cp command)

You can copy files to a USB drive and copy them manually to the hard drive from the command line using the `cp` command. This way is *not* recommended because it's cumbersome, easy to mistype something, and can be confusing about the mount point for the usb drive. It's just not the easiest way:

```
cp /mnt/usbdrive/My_Movie.avi /mydrive/Movies/My_Movie.avi
```

or for a folder:

```
cp "/mnt/usbdrive/Land of the Lost" "/mydrive/TV/Land for the Lost"
```

Note that quotation marks are required if any part of the filename or folder name contains spaces.

Using a Text-Mode File Manager installed on the Pi (Midnight Commander or mc)

You can copy the files using a text-mode file manager like Midnight Commander. Midnight Commander is a visual file manager that you can install with the following commands:

```
sudo apt install mc
```

And then run the app by typing **mc** at the command line. This is much easier than simply typing commands from the command line, but the Midnight Commander program has a million little features, and it may be a challenge in its own right. I do recommend that you install and play around with it. It's really useful for renaming, deleting, and moving files around your system later on if the need arises.

Use FileZilla to FTP from another Computer

This is the way I usually do it, and I recommend this for most people.

From another computer, you can use a graphical FTP (*File Transfer Protocol*) program to copy files to the Raspberry Pi's hard drive from somewhere else on your home network. This is the easiest and most intuitive way to get your files copied, but since it's done through your network, it's going to be a little slower than copying right from a USB drive.

1. First, download and install the FileZilla app on another computer on your network; the app is available in versions for Windows, Mac, and Linux, so whatever computer you have, you should be able to find a working version of it. The app and installation instructions can be found at:

```
https://filezilla-project.org/
```

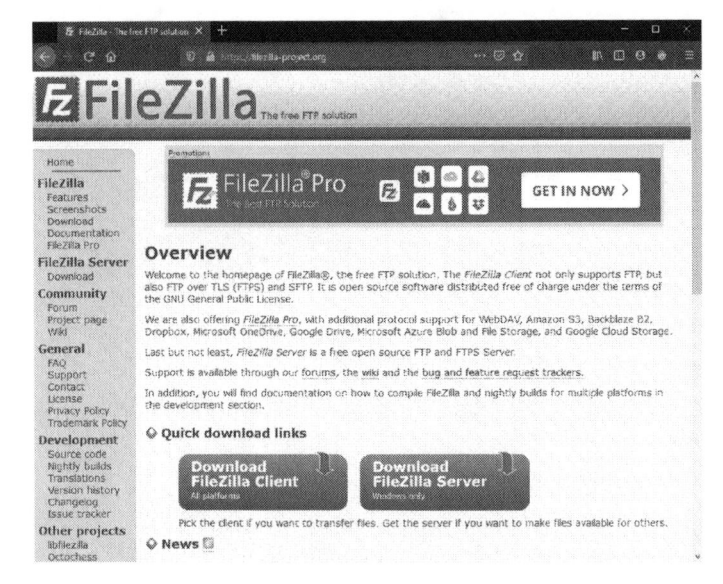

Filezilla Download Page

2. Once you have installed FileZilla, run it. You'll see the main window of the app, looking something like this:

Building a Plex Server with Raspberry Pi   65

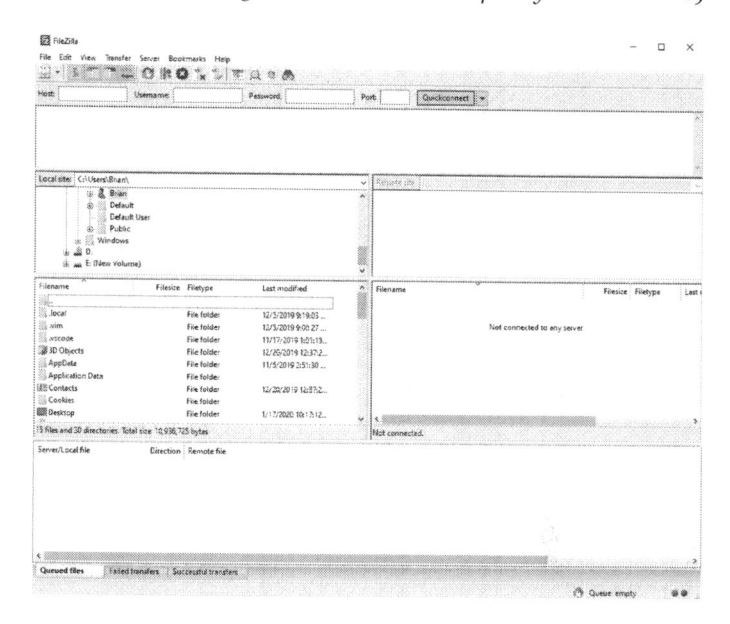

There's a lot here that we don't need to know right away, but you can look at the various options and learn the app fully if you want to later on. For now, all we need to do is use FileZilla to log into the Raspberry Pi. At the top of the app's window, just below the main toolbar, are little input fields where you can type in:

- **Host:** This is your Plex Server's IP address. Mine is at 192.168.0.6
- **Username:** This is the user "pi" unless you used something else.
- **Password:** This is whatever you changed it to earlier. If you are still using the default password (shame on you!) the default is "raspberry"
- **Port:** The port number is 22

Here's mine filled in:

Filezilla "Quick Connect" Boxes

The password field doesn't display when you type it in, so be careful that you typed it correctly. Hit `Enter` on the keyboard or click on the "`Quickconnect`" button. Assuming everything is correct, you should see something like this:

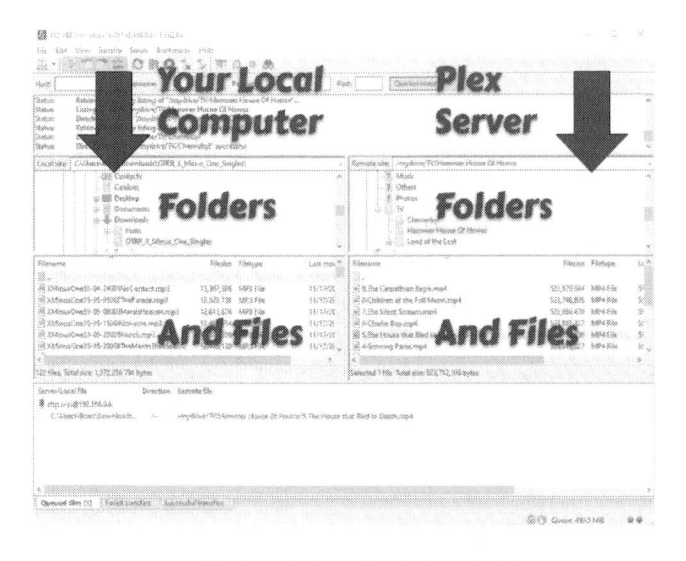

Filezilla In Action, with windows labeled

For the moment, ignore the top and bottom panes. The four windows on the left and right sides are what's important right now.

The top-left window is the folder/directory structure on your local computer. You use this window to browse to wherever your media files are currently stored. This could be your Downloads folder, your Photo or Music Folder, somewhere on an external drive, or wherever you put your media files. Once you point this window to the proper folder, the files within that folder will appear in the window just beneath it.

The top-right window is the same thing, but for the folders on your Raspberry Pi. Move through the folders in the top window until the destination folder is visible. At least in the beginning, there probably won't be any files in the destination folder.

If you see a file in the lower-left window that you want to copy to the Plex server, then you can either double-click it or drag it to the window on the right. You can watch the status of the transfer in the window on the bottom of the app. If you right-click on a file, you can rename it, delete, add it to an upload queue, or a host of other options that you can figure out later if you choose.

This is not a book on FileZilla, but keep in mind there are many other functions that you may want to learn if you are going to be using the app a lot. You can select and add more than one file or folder at a time, you can set up a transfer queue that will run without you needing to be present, and you can set up the "Site Manager" so that you don't have to enter login information every time you load FileZilla. For the Site Manager, just pull down the File Menu and choose "Site Manager." You'll see something like this:

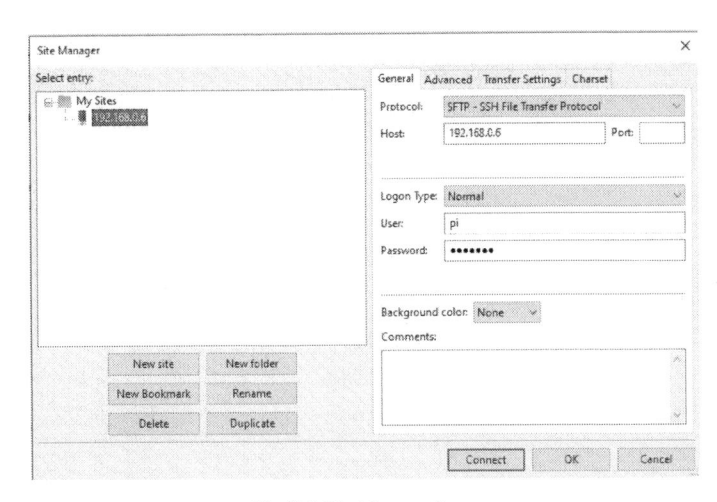

Filezilla's Site Manager Screen

You can create a "New Site" on the left, then enter your login information on the right, and in the future you can use it to connect without all that typing. It's very handy. I strongly recommend spending some time and learning what FileZilla can do-- I spend a lot of time transferring files with it, and if you do any kind of "other networking stuff" at all, it can quickly become indispensable.

The next job is the time-consuming one: copy all your media files to the Plex Media folders you already set up.

As before, in your browser's URL bar, you can type: **http://192.168.0.6:32400/web** or **https://app.plex.tv** to log into the Plex server.

6

CONFIGURING THE PLEX MEDIA SERVER

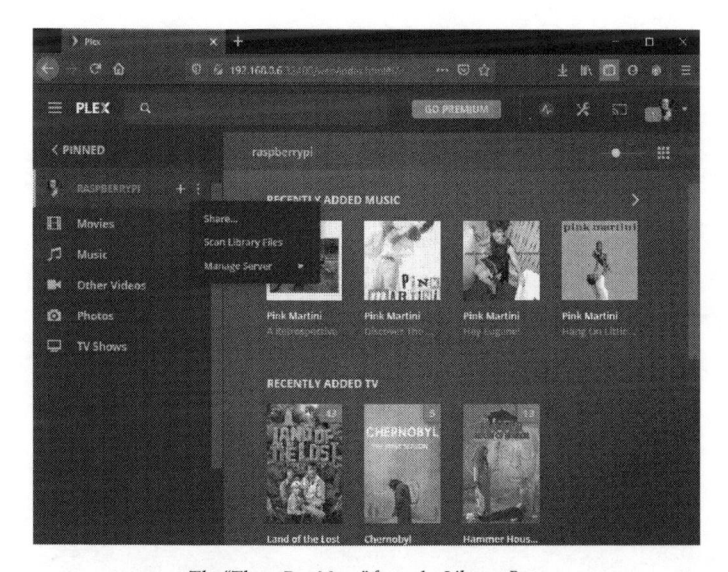

The "Three-Dot Menu" from the Library Pane

The Main Plex Screen

Depending on how you have Plex set up, your shows and

music might just start automatically appearing within the Plex interface as shown above.

If nothing appears after a few minutes, then you'll need to tell the system scan for new media that has been added. You'll see "raspberrypi" (or whatever you named your Plex server if you changed the name) in orange type on the left section of the screen. If you hover your mouse over that text, a "plus sign" and a "three-dots menu" will appear. The plus sign allows you to add new media folders and libraries. The three dots allow you to:

Share...

The sharing feature allows you to send an email to someone, and they will be able to access your media files. You can also specify exactly what they can access: only movies, only TV shows, or whatever combination of libraries you assign them.

Scan Library Files

is the one we want if the media doesn't start showing up after you've finished copying files to the appropriate folders. Click on this, and Plex will scan through all the media folders and add in anything new since the last time the scan was performed. We'll see later how to automate this process. Note that once your library starts getting big, this can take quite a while.

Manage Server... Has a submenu with four tools:

> **Settings**
>
> **Empty Trash** - When you delete a media file, it doesn't really go away immediately. Just like the trash can on your

computer desktop, "removed" files get held in a trash can. The trash can gets deleted automatically after some period of time, but you can empty it manually if you wish.

Optimize Database You probably won't need this anytime soon. Every time you add a new file, a database listing is created. When you delete a file, that database doesn't go away. After you've run the system for a long time, and added and deleted a huge number of files, the database may start to get bogged down. This function cleans things up for you.

Clean Bundles Similar to Optimize Database above, this feature goes through and deletes any metadata (images, descriptions, covert art, etc.) that were once associated with a media file that has since been deleted.

Clicking on the various Libraries beneath the machine name will show you only the media files that go with that type; only Movies, or only Music, etc.

For the most part, the Plex interface is really intuitive, but it wouldn't hurt to go over some of the main elements. In the left-hand pane of the Plex window, you see a list of libraries.

Home

This is where you'll find the most recent files that have been added to Plex, the shows you've only halfway finished, and if you scroll down, you will find recent news stories, online videos, and podcasts to which you have subscribed. Most of the controls and buttons allow you to hover your mouse over them for hints as to what they do.

Movies

This tab is where you'll find the files you sorted into the Movies folder. You should see thumbnails, titles, and release dates of the movies you've put into Plex. At the top of the screen, you'll find tabs for Recommended, Library, and Collections.

Recommended movies are new releases and movies that you have recently added to Plex.

Library is where you'll find all your movies, and on the line below the tabs, you'll see options for All, Movies, and Title. "All" lets you filter the movies based on certain criteria; for example, you can list just movies released in 2013 if you choose. "Movies" lets you toggle between the standard movie view and a list of folders. "By Title" allows you to sort the onscreen list of movies by various criteria.

Collections are set up by tagging movies as a collection, and you can create your own groups of films, say just the Harry Potter films, into a collection.

TV Shows

Contains essentially the same filtering and sorting features as the Movies library, except instead of the release year, Plex shows how many seasons of the show you have as well as how old the most recent episode is.

Music

Again the same basic menus, but the music category tells

you the Artist/Group name and the name of the album, along with the album art.

Photos

Offers the options for "Recommended," "Timeline," and "Library."

Recommended gives you various other listings such as recently added photos or photos from a specific year or decade.

Timeline shows all your photos sorted by date.

Library shows all your photos in various other ways, sortable by your own criteria.

Tidal

Tidal is a music streaming service offered by Plex. This is not free, and also not part of the Plex Pass. This is a completely additional service. In the show description for many movies and TV shows, songs that appear in the shows and soundtrack titles will be listed below the "Play" controls. You can preview a sample of these songs for free, but you would need to subscribe to Tidal to hear the whole soundtrack.

News

News shows tabs at the top of the screen for Recommended, Categories, and Channels. "Recommended" are top news stories, local news (if you have personalized the news settings), and other recommended news videos. The option for "Categories" lets you show business news, gaming news, sports, world news, and other topical content. The "Channels" tab shows actual channels like USA Today, Bloomberg, Reuters, the Financial Times, and so forth. The three-dots allow you to personalize your favorite topics and put in your local postal code for local news.

Podcasts

Podcasts are free, audio-only shows that cover any imaginable kind of topic. As with News, the three dots allow you to personalize your choices. The "Recommended" tab lists your uncompleted episodes and other shows you might be interested in. "My Podcasts" will list the shows you are subscribed to. New episodes of your favorite shows will automatically be placed here. "Categories" are an easy way to browse podcast topics that may interest you.

Web Shows

Web shows, as far as Plex is concerned, are essentially video podcasts. You subscribe to them in the same way, and the menus work the same way.

Important Settings

The Plex server settings can be found at any time by clicking on the "wrench-and-screwdriver" icon near the top-right of most Plex screens. There are a large number of settings and options, and to be honest, most of them you will never need to adjust unless you start running into problems. Still, we should go over the important ones now:

Remote Access - This is where you enable people from outside your network to be able to access your media. If you never plan to watch your media outside the house, then it's going to be safer to turn this off. If you know you will be watching your media away from the house, then turn this on.

Agents - This has tabs for Movies, Shows, Artist, Albums, and Photos. Each of these tabs lists various "agents" or online databases. You can select where Plex gets metadata like album art, playlists, movie stars and crew, seasons for TV shows, and similar information. I would recommend turning on *all* the various sources. If you start running into problems with one of the sources, then you can turn them off one by one if necessary.

Library - This allows you to tell Plex how often to scan for new media additions. "Scan my library automatically," "Run a partial scan when changes are detected," "Include music libraries in automatic updates" are all good things to turn on. Actually, I have all these options turned on except for the "Scan my library periodically" option, since it seems redundant since I have scan automatically turned on.

Languages - Set this to your primary language, and turn on the options to automatically use that language's audio and/or subtitles. Note that you can turn on or off subtitles and choose audio tracks for each movie when it's time to play the film, assuming your media files support multiple languages and you have the subtitle files.

More - The settings and features in Plex are extremely numerous, and most of them only need adjustment in case of some kind of failure. Still, it's a good idea to skim through the various options and see what's there (new features are added regularly). The official documentation for these settings can be found at

```
https://support.plex.tv/articles/200289408-
plex-web-app-settings/
```

7
BACKING UP YOUR SD CARD

By this point, you've put a lot of work into getting your Raspberry Pi computer all set up. You've got Wi-Fi passwords entered, and you have an external drive configured. You've built a Plex library with potentially tens of thousands of audio and video files. It'd be a shame if something happened to all that work!

Hard drives are pretty reliable, and you've already got all your important media files on an external hard drive. In this case, the weak point is the SD card with the operating system and all that Plex data. SD cards do tend to get corrupted from time to time. Once in a while, it's a good idea to make a backup of the SD card that contains your operating system and all the apps and configuration data stored on it. That way, if something does corrupt the card, you can just restore your configured settings and system right over it, and since your personal media will be stored on the hard drive, nothing important will be lost. If it's been a while since your last backup, you can always use "scan my media files" to update the Plex database with recently-added stuff after a restore.

To back up the SD card, you will once again need another computer, along with whatever adaptor you may need to plug the SD card into it.

Shutdown your Raspberry Pi using the following command:

```
sudo shutdown
```

And when everything stops, turn off the power to the Pi. Next, remove the SD card and move to your computer for the next steps.

From a Mac:

1. Bring up a terminal window, but do not plug in the SD card yet.

2. Type: `diskutil list`

3. Insert the SD card.

4. Now type that same command again:

```
diskutil list
```

and note the new drive name that appears. This is the SD Card name/number.

5. In the terminal, type the following, replacing the *x* in *rdiskx* with whatever the disk number is that you found in step 6:

```
sudo dd if=/dev/rdiskx of=./backup_file.dmg
```

Building a Plex Server with Raspberry Pi

6. This can take a very long time (My card took nearly an hour), and there is no feedback from the program until it's completely finished. Be patient!

Someday, if you need to restore the card:

1. Figure out the disk number by repeating steps 1-4 above.
2. Type the following, replacing the *x* in *rdiskx* with whatever your SD card's drive is numbered:

```
diskutil unmountDisk /dev/rdiskx
sudo dd if=./backup_file.dmg of=/dev/rdiskx
sudo diskutil eject /dev/rdiskx
```

From Windows:

1. Download and install the **Win32DiskImager** App from https://sourceforge.net/projects/win32diskimager/files/latest/download
2. Insert the SD Card.
3. Run Win32DiskImager, and then choose both the location where you want to create the backup file and the name of the SD card.
4. Click "Read" to begin copying.
5. This can take a very long time, but you can watch progress bar as shown in Figure 2-3

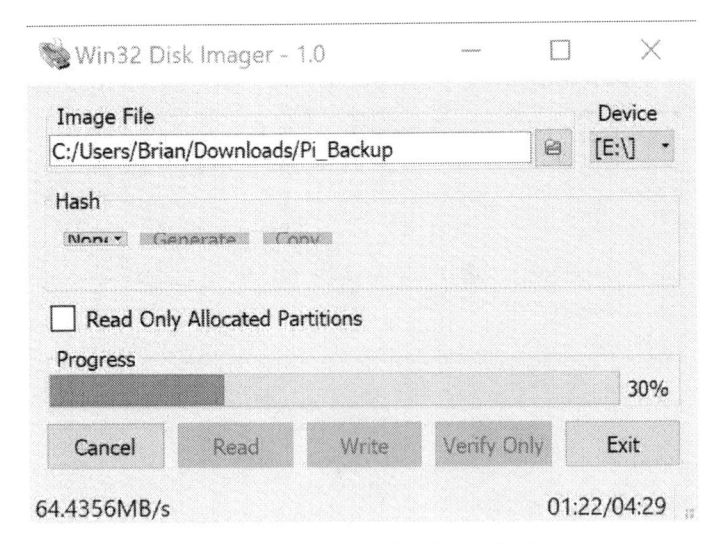

Win32DiskImager Reading the SD Card

If, at some point, you need to restore the SD card from your backup, just run Win32DiskImager, choose the backup file and the SD Card drive letter, and choose "Write" instead of "Read" in the steps above to run the process in reverse.

8

BACKING UP YOUR HARD DRIVE(S)

Just like with Windows or MacOS, there are various ways to backup your hard drives. The simplest way to backup your external hard drive is to simply

1. Shutdown your RPI
2. Unplug the hard drive
3. Plug the drive into another computer
4. Copy or backup the drive in whatever system or app that you're already familiar with using on that computer.

It's also possible to plug in a second external hard drive and mirror your media drive to that new drive using the dd command. If you go back to the section where we installed your first hard drive, you can once again use the sudo fdisk command with the list (L menu option) to view all the attached drive names. You already know the drive name of your media drive (in our earlier example, it was */dev/sda1*). You will also need to plug in and figure out the drive name of the blank, target drive (possibly */dev/sdb1*, but it could be something else). Once you know the two drive/partition names, you can use the dd command like this:

```
sudo dd if=<input device name> of=<output device name>
```

Substituting your drive names for the source and destination drives. For example, if your working Media drive is *sda1*, and your backup drive is *sdb1*, then you would type:

```
sudo dd if=/dev/sda1 of=/dev/sdb1
```

Note that one (only partially joking) name for the dd command is "disk destroyer." If you get the two drives backwards, it'll overwrite your media with whatever's on the second drive, which is probably not what you want. Be very careful with this command. More information can be found at:

```
https://opensource.com/article/18/7/how-use-dd-linux
```

9
USING THE PLEX MEDIA SERVER

Setting up the Plex server can be a bit tedious, but not especially tricky. If you've organized your files properly, if you've set up the app to look up all the metadata from the proper agents, and if you've managed to upload your movies, TV shows, and music into the right folders, then it's time to enjoy the show!

You can watch Plex media from any computer, tablet device, smartphone, smartTV, or any other device that can run either a Plex App or a Web Browser.

From a Computer or Web Browser

We've already logged into the web browser by using your IP number:

192.168.0.6:32400/web/

(substituting your own IP number)

or

https://app.plex.tv

That's all there is to starting Plex on your Chromebook, PC, Mac, Linux, or any other device running a web browser. Don't forget that most web browsers can be set to go into full screen mode if necessary (Usually by hitting the F11 Key on the keyboard if you have one).

The image below is my fully-populated Plex server looking at the overview for a TV Show. I already chose the series I want to watch, "Doctor Who," and now it wants me to select which season/series I want to see. Once I select a season, I will need to select a specific episode. Note that if the series is "unwatched" it will default to Season 1, Episode 1, and then continue on to episode 2, playing all the episodes in the proper sequence. It will remember the movies and TV episodes you've already watched, so you don't have to remember.

Information screen for a TV Series - Web Browser View

Tablets and Phones

You *can* run Plex on a smartphone or tablet using that device's browser, but you'll probably get a better experience running one of the Apps made specifically for that device. For Android, iPhone, and iPads, just go to the appropriate App Store and install the Plex app. Generally, once you have downloaded the app, it will ask for your Plex email and password, and then it'll take care of everything else for you.

Here are a few screenshots from my iPad Mini running Plex:

Information screen for a TV Series - iPad Mini View

The above shot is the tablet version of the same series as shown in the earlier web view. The information and options are all the same, but the interface is quite a bit different.

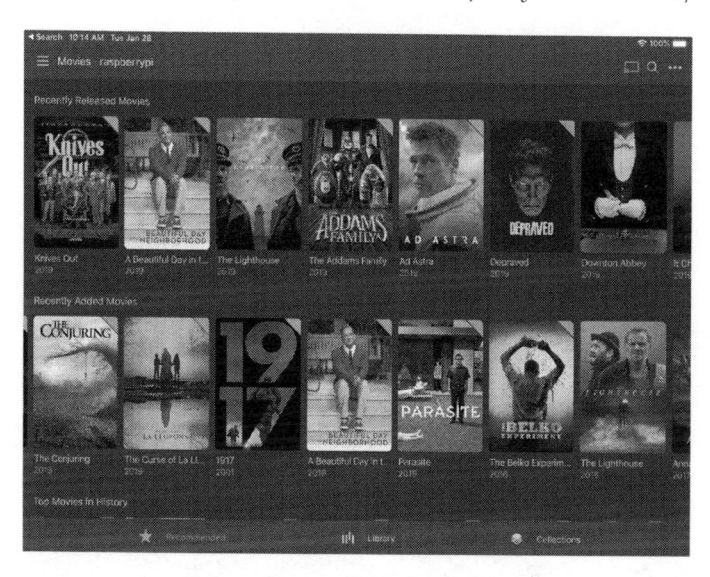

Information screen for Movies - iPad View

The above is the screen you get on the iPad when you click on "Movies." The first row shows recently released movies, based on the film's theatrical release date. The second row shows movies that were recently added to Plex. In the shot above, "Knives Out" was released more recently than "The Conjuring," even though I added "The Conjuring" more recently than "Knives Out".

Beneath the two rows in the above screenshot (not shown, you'd need to scroll down in Plex) are "Recently Played Movies," "Top Unplayed Movies" (highly rated by other viewers), and other categories that depend on what you've recently added or watched (these are unpredictable).

Next up, a few screenshots of what you can expect in Music. It starts out showing the albums you've recently played in case you want to hear them again. This is followed by recently added music. These are followed by other albums in the same genre, your most-played music, and possibly information about artists on tour. All of these are based completely on what's in your library and what you listen to.

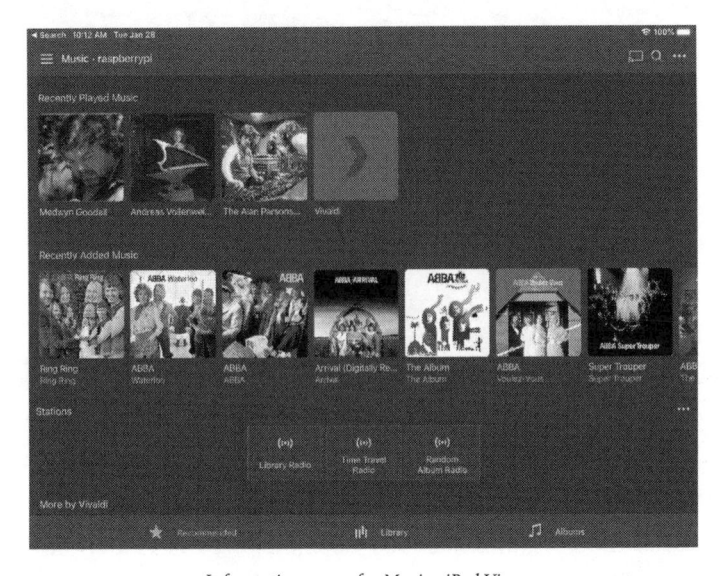

Information screen for Music - iPad View

If you click on an album, you get the following screen. You can start to play on track one, add it to a playlist, go to the album listing, where you can choose to play individual songs, go to the Artist page, which lists only songs and albums from that artist, or you can download the songs from the Plex server to your device for offline use.

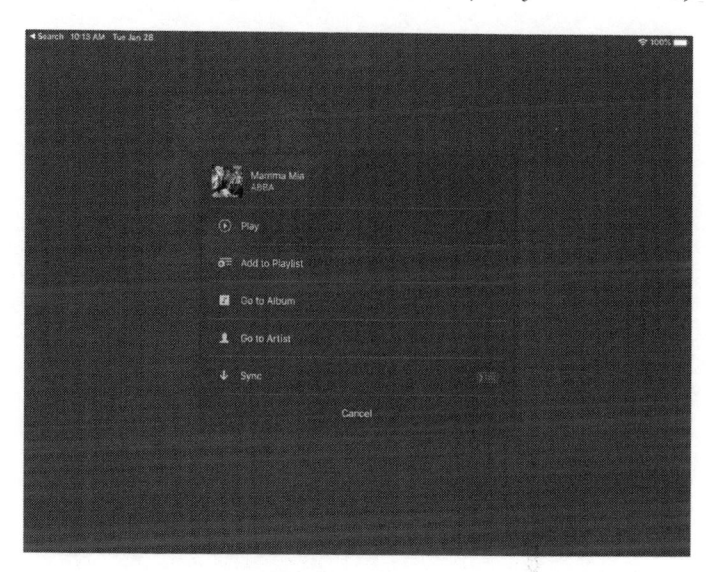

Control screen for Music - iPad View

Next up is the album screen. In the shot below, I have selected the "Mamma Mia" album by Abba. You get the cover art, along with buttons to "Add to Playlist", "shuffle songs," "Play," "Download," and "See more options." You also have the option of selecting just a single song to play:

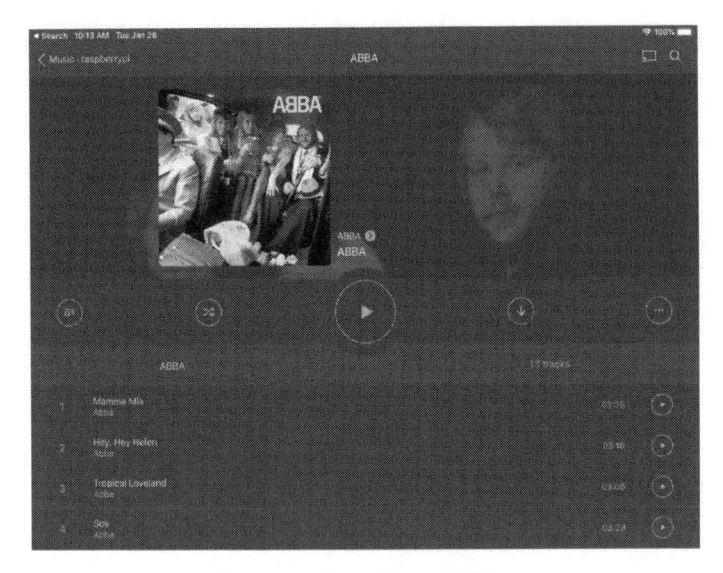

Player screen for an Album - iPad View

Although the above shots are from the iPad, both iPhone and Android interfaces work similarly and are designed to be intuitive and easy to use.

SmartTV Options

The experience for smart TV devices is much like that of the tablet, only on a bigger screen. The screenshots below are from the Apple TV, but other systems look similar. Here is a photo of the same shows as above on the living room TV:

Photo of the TV Series Overview Page - Apple TV View

And of the list of available TV Shows:

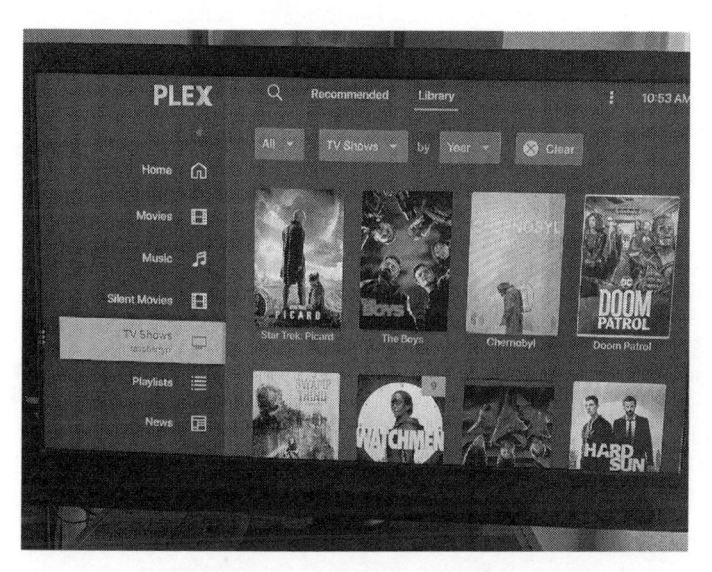

Photo of the TV Series Listing Page - Apple TV View

As you can see, no matter what device you use to consume the media on your Plex server, the interface is pretty consistent.

10
CONCLUSION

And that is about all there is to it. Plex is continually adding new features and settings, so I haven't gone into the weeds too much on the technical settings. What we've covered here will get you set up and running, but there's still quite a bit of fine-tuning and customizing that you can do. Setting up new categories, playlists, and getting everything tweaked just right can be rewarding, but is not strictly necessary if you just want to watch your movies. Also remember, Plex can play literally hundreds of thousands of podcasts and free web shows with no cost or work on your part other than selecting which shows you like.

Everything we've done in this book was with the free version of Plex. We never really looked into the "Plex Pass," but Plex is regularly adding new shows and benefits for paying customers. One additional benefit is the ability to download and watch media *offline* on your remote devices, which is quite nice. It's certainly worth your time to look into paying for the service, but it's truly not necessary for just basic media serving.

In the future, keep in mind that you can always add additional external hard drives, or even connect to a NAS or other file storage system. If you have crazy-fast Internet access, you might even be able to use cloud storage for your movies. You can watch your media from anywhere on your home network and consume no Internet bandwidth, but watching them outside the house does use a lot of data, both on your phone/device and from the household server, so make sure you have a data plan that can cover it.

And of course, the heart of the system is the Raspberry Pi, the tiny little inexpensive computer. The Raspberry Pi as a device has come a long way in just a few short years. Once just a device for electronics nerds, now it's a full, completely usable computer for many types of projects that once required a full-sized PC. The Plex Media Server is just one of a vast number of projects for which you can use these little devices. May people use a Raspberry Pi for one project, for example, a Plex Media Server, and then end up getting more of them for other things, like a home NAS, a music jukebox, "Magic Mirror," and hundreds of other applications, not to mention as a complete desktop replacement. If this last idea intrigues you, I should point out that I have also written "Computing with the Raspberry Pi: Command Line and GUI Linux (Technology in Action)" available through Apress Publishing, which is all about using the Pi as a desktop replacement. You *can* do it!

Good luck with your Pi, and have loads of fun with your Plex Server!

ABOUT THE AUTHOR

I am a former College IT Instructor with an extensive background in computers dating back to the 1980s. Currently, I write on a wide array of topics from computers, to world religions, to ham radio, and I've even released an occasional short horror tale.

∼

I'd love to hear your stories of success and failure with the Raspberry Pi and Plex Media Server software. If there's something you would like to see in a future edition of the book, or otherwise have suggestions, please drop me a note.

Contact me at:

> Web: http://BrianSchell.com
> Email: brian@brianschell.com

Also, please join my email update list— There's NO weekly SPAM or filler material, only announcements of new books or major updates.

Email update link: http://brianschell.com/list/

If you have a suggestion or find a mistake, email me about it, and I'll get it into an updated edition of the book. Got a gripe, complaint, question, or just adoring fan mail? Same thing!

Leave a Review

If this book helped you, please leave a review where you purchased this book. Reviews are the best way to help out!

Share With Your Friends

Did you enjoy this book? Please use the buttons below to spread the word to your friends and followers.

Share on Facebook

Share on Twitter

twitter.com/BrianSchell
facebook.com/Brian.Schell
instagram.com/brian_schell
pinterest.com/brianschell

ALSO BY BRIAN SCHELL

Amateur Radio

- D-Star for Beginners
- Echolink for Beginners
- DMR for Beginners Using the Tytera MD-380
- SDR for Beginners with the SDRPlay
- Programming Amateur Radios with CHIRP
- FM Satellite Communications for Beginners
- Trunking Scanners for Beginners Using the Uniden TrunkTracker

Technology

- Going Chromebook: Living in the Cloud
- Going Chromebook: Mastering Google Docs
- Going Chromebook: Mastering Google Sheets
- Computing with the Raspberry Pi: Command Line and GUI Linux (Technology in Action)
- Going Text: Mastering the Power of the Command Line
- Going iPad: Ditching the Desktop
- DOS Today: Running Vintage MS-DOS Games and Apps on a Modern Computer

Old-Time Radio Listener's Guides

- OTR Listener's Guide to Dark Fantasy
- OTR Listener's Guide to Box 13

The Five-Minute Buddhist Series

- The Five-Minute Buddhist
- The Five-Minute Buddhist Returns
- The Five-Minute Buddhist Meditates
- The Five-Minute Buddhist's Quick Start Guide to Buddhism
- Teaching and Learning in Japan: An English Teacher Abroad

Fiction with Kevin L. Knights:

- Tales to Make You Shiver
- Tales to Make You Shiver 2
- Random Acts of Cloning
- Jess and the Monsters

Made in the USA
Monee, IL
29 May 2024